GW00467533

# JOURNEY THROUGH THE GUILT TRIP

# JOURNEY THROUGH THE GUILT TRIP

*Creating A Positive Relationship with Guilt and A Life You Love*

*Lee Lam*

www.journeythroughtheguilttrip.co.uk

*For my husband Steve, for putting up with me writing into the early hours of the morning and for the continuous mugs of coffee. And for Morgan and Lexi, my beautiful daughters who make every day worthwhile. I hope that you are as proud of me as I am of you.*

*xxx*

# Contents

enough for me to stop the conversation with them – they want to also convince me to stop having the conversation with *anyone*. The hurt or pain brought up by the emotion is too much and they do not understand that it is *that* pain and hurt which is exactly the reason I talk about it.

That's why I'm always encouraged by those who give me my third and favourite response – they are my kind of people. To these individuals, when I mention guilt, you see the vulnerability, the uncertainty, the slight stiffening of the back as if getting ready to fight or flee – and then they say, "tell me more". These are my warriors – those who are willing to ease their way through the discomfort to find out what is on the other side.

They usually have been on a course of self-discovery for a while, trying to find the elusive reason behind how they feel, whether that is joy-less, fearful, anxious, depressed, under loved, or under confident. Whilst there are many ways of understanding how to get out of it, they know that these techniques are not solving the fundamental reasons, and as I frame my concept of guilt to them, the light goes on and suddenly the pieces fall into place. At the heart of all of their doubts and fears is the guilt that somehow, they are getting life wrong – and they don't know what to do about it.

But guilt doesn't always look like guilt. It's incredibly adept in its ability to distract and divert focus from itself and into another emotion that looks like it is more useful yet keeps you from solving the underlying issue. Sometimes it shows itself as confusion or frustration, irritation that you just can't get things to make any sense. Sometimes it feels like you are lost, like you have no sense of direction or focus, and you can't trust yourself to go the right way. And sometimes, it makes you wonder why you are here at all.

### 18 years ago
I'm sitting on a sofa, but I can't feel it. I could have been sitting on an ice-cold stone floor and I wouldn't have noticed. I'm fascinated with the in and out movement of my chest and the rhythm of my breath. I'm trying hard to block out my own thoughts by focusing on that breath. Because no matter how hard I try, the only thoughts I hear are coming from a voice that keeps repeating "*That's it, time's up. You were supposed to be perfect and you're not. So, time's up - let*

# Contents

# 1: Introduction

G uilt is not something that many people are eager to admit to or look at too closely. It's uncomfortable, loaded with potential pain and vulnerability, and just mentioning it tends to bring out a range of reactions.

I've seen the whole spectrum when I explain that I work with guilt. The first reaction I get is the poker face. As I talk, I'm met with a blank face – you know the blank face that can only be pulled by *really* intentionally freezing all parts of your face at the same time? They are aiming for what looks like a neutral response, closely aligned with "I have no emotional response for what you've just said because it matters so little to me". But I see the fear in their eyes that I'm going to somehow climb into their hidden shadowy closet and pull out a skeleton or two. That's not what I do, but I can understand their reservation.

Another common reaction is the denial. They can't quite manage a full poker face so instead, they decide to try and convince me that they do not, nor ever have, felt guilty, ever at all, in their whole entire life. In fact, most of them will go on to explain to me what a ridiculous subject it is to talk about, how it is a ploy to make people (i.e. them) uncomfortable and I should be ashamed of myself for using such a word. It's too negative, it weakens people and how can it help to make people focus on it? I don't blame these people at all for the hostility – guilt is the emotion that convinces you that there is a problem with *you*, that there is something wrong with *you*, and so naturally your mind is going to put up defences against that onslaught.

What's always interesting to me is just how animated they are while they are telling me that they don't feel anything at all. And it's not enough for me to stop the conversation with them – they want to also convince me to stop having the conversation with *anyone*. The hurt or pain brought up by the emotion is too much and they do not understand that it is *that* pain and hurt which is exactly the reason I talk about it.

That's why I'm always encouraged by those who give me my third and favourite response – they are my kind of people. To these individuals, when I mention guilt, you see the vulnerability, the uncertainty, the slight stiffening of the back as if getting ready to fight or flee – and then they say, "tell me more". These are my warriors – those who are willing to ease their way through the discomfort to find out what is on the other side.

They usually have been on a course of self-discovery for a while, trying to find the elusive reason behind how they feel, whether that is joy-less, fearful, anxious, depressed, under loved, or under confident. Whilst there are many ways of understanding how to get out of it, they know that these techniques are not solving the fundamental reasons, and as I frame my concept of guilt to them, the light goes on and suddenly the pieces fall into place. At the heart of all of their doubts and fears is the guilt that somehow, they are getting life wrong – and they don't know what to do about it.

But guilt doesn't always look like guilt. It's incredibly adept in its ability to distract and divert focus from itself and into another emotion that looks like it is more useful yet keeps you from solving the underlying issue. Sometimes it shows itself as confusion or frustration, irritation that you just can't get things to make any sense. Sometimes it feels like you are lost, like you have no sense of direction or focus, and you can't trust yourself to go the right way. And sometimes, it makes you wonder why you are here at all.

### 18 years ago
I'm sitting on a sofa, but I can't feel it. I could have been sitting on an ice-cold stone floor and I wouldn't have noticed. I'm fascinated with the in and out movement of my chest and the rhythm of my breath. I'm trying hard to block out my own thoughts by focusing on that breath. Because no matter how hard I try, the only thoughts I hear are coming from a voice that keeps repeating "*That's it, time's up. You were supposed to be perfect and you're not. So, time's up - let*

*someone else try. You're not needed or wanted any more. Nobody will notice you not being around – why would they?"*

Do I want to die? Dear God, no – there is a faint, almost indiscernible other voice which seemed to be coming from my stomach, screaming "What the f*** are you talking about?!? Who even are you??!?" But the calm, monotone voice keeps repeating it – *"Time's up, you've screwed up, you got it wrong, you are wrong. Time to go."* While I'm silently screaming that it's talking utter bullshit and there is no way that I agree with it, it is winning the war in my brain, and its power starts to take over my body, until my thoughts move from should I to how to.

Looking back, I'm incredibly grateful that my family saw that something wasn't right before I acted upon any of those impulses or had given into that voice. They didn't know everything that was going on in my head that day, but they did see that I had completely disconnected from reality, and that I needed help. I remember sitting in the doctor's office, my mum by my side, and feeling like a spectator as I was assessed as a suicide risk. I answered the questions honestly because I just didn't have the capacity to lie. The way in which I was able to answer such life changing words so dispassionately and calmly frightened me – and yet I couldn't even muster fear. I didn't resonate with what I was saying *at all* – I knew that it wasn't really me - and yet I understood it was coming from a part of me that was done being suppressed under years of guilt, triggered by trying to be the best I could be, in line with the rules of what others said were right. I was too focused on trying to live up to the image of me that had been built up over my lifetime. And I had failed.

The doctor, after asking his questions, gave me anti-depressants, which I thank him for. For me, the little white pills acted like a plaster cast on a broken leg. It allowed parts of my brain to pause and rest, to stop functioning and most importantly, to stop thinking. What I needed most of all was to take a break while my internal brain chatter and turbulent emotions quietened and healed. It is easy to forget that anti-depressants don't just stop the negative emotions. They work by stopping your ability to feel anything. And in that moment, that was blessed relief. I didn't – couldn't - feel anything. Even finding something funny hurt – it required my brain to run through so many of the rules of what *was* funny – about what was right or wrong, what

I could do, what I should do – should I even find that funny? I was overloaded to the point of pain.

Over my life, I had been trying to be 'more' and I had written an encyclopaedic list in my mind of what I could and couldn't do, what I should or shouldn't do, in order to gain acceptance, to be included, to be loved or wanted. These rules - as you can imagine – were complex and the vast majority of them contradicted each other. They had been created by listening to everyone who I ever interacted with, and I would find out what the rules were for them – then I would try to live by those rules, feeling guilty if I couldn't achieve the same results.

As I grew older, that number increased by so much and the rules became so radically different, that I would follow one rule and feel guilty about not following the equal and opposite rule that I also had in my head. Just like a computer that has been given a piece of code that simply wasn't logical, I very quickly self-destructed, leading to the mental equivalent of the blue screen of death on a PC. I had created so many rules, and so many of them were at odds with each other, that my brain was no longer able to process them and use them effectively. To continue to use computer terms, I needed a reboot. That is what the anti-depressants provided me – time to get my head straight, to get the rule book purged and to find a way of creating new ones that I felt mentally comfortable with.

At the time, it was a relief to have emotions and feelings silenced, but there was always a part of me that knew that it wasn't really 'living' - it wasn't even really surviving but more *existing*. With nothing else to put my mind to, with no more feelings to have to process, I was no longer hurting but I was no longer doing or feeling *anything*. In the still of the night, my breath once more became the only thing that made me feel that I was still alive and in control.

How had I got to this point? Why had I created this rule book and why was it so confusing? Where did I even get these rules from? I realized that the only way I was going to be able to rewrite the code and to rewrite the rule book was to examine each one closely and work out why it was there, who had put it there, and was it one that I wanted?

To do this, I needed to go back, right to the beginning.

Growing up, I was smart. I saw patterns and trends and logic before many of those around me, and I revelled in it. I memorised all of the questions in Trivial Pursuit (when it launched there were about 6000 questions in the box) and I would read anything and everything, from the back of cereal boxes to War and Peace. I recognized almost immediately that I got praise (and most importantly, attention) from adults for doing well, so I focused on doing better and better. Some children would misbehave to get attention and focus, but for me, it was my knowledge and my intellect – and most importantly, it was my insistence that you follow the rules.

The problem came when I seemed to have a different set of rules than other children around me. As I went up in my teachers' estimations, I went down in my classmates'. I became an answers machine for them, useful for when they wanted the answer without much effort, but otherwise a slightly strange, odd girl who would say and do things that didn't fit with how I was supposed to act. As school children do everywhere, they made sure I knew I was different, that I wasn't following their rules and that this gave them a reason to ignore me or shun me. If I laughed at a joke, they announced that it wasn't funny. If I started to play a game with them, they changed the rules of the game that would mean I couldn't play. When providing the answers, I was no longer being helpful but fulfilling the indisputable obligation to provide them.

As I grew older the rules became more sophisticated and try as I might I could never catch up with them. Whenever I thought I knew the rules, they would change. I could never learn the game, I could never feel certain that I was visible, or that I was accepted, as the rules for such inclusion remained elusive and complicated. If I kept one person happy, someone else would feel bad and I would be racked with guilt that I had yet again got the rules wrong. For someone who prided herself on her ability to know every answer, how could I get so many of these rules wrong? In the end, it was easier to hang about with the teachers because their rules didn't seem to shift as much.

My story is heartbreakingly common. When you try to fit in, but the social group you want to fit into does not want to accept you as you are, you feel guilty as you try to work out what you have done wrong. There appears to be a simple choice – keep trying to understand and play by their rules or remain on the outside.

My only route into that social grouping was with my intelligence and my ability to finish my work so quickly I had time to do everyone else's. I always used to say that I never competed with anyone at my school, college or university – I was only ever in competition with myself, to get better and better. It is only once I hit this breaking point that I truly understood that the competition I had with myself was to see if I could finally get acknowledged and visible. It had nothing to do with whether I could get top marks. In my rule book, the two had slowly merged into one.

As a child, you look around you at what others are doing, to try to work out what you need to do as well. Your role models aren't clearly described as such, so it becomes any of the adults that you see or interact with. You see people getting praised or criticised depending on their actions and whilst you may be able to immediately tell why, in most cases it is actually a really grey area. The same action can make one person happy and another angry – so who is right? Most importantly, which one will accept you and make you feel wanted or seen? The need to belong predisposes you to feeling guilty for not conforming to what is accepted, but everyone seems to expect different things; in some cases, completely rejecting any of the other alternatives. Guilt is the emotion that lives between a rock and a hard place.

It is this constant conflict, fed by a need for connection and social interaction, that allows the likes of street gangs or cults to become a viable option for a lot of people. They know that they are not necessarily offering a better option, but they are offering social inclusion as a consequence of following their particular rules. Other social groupings aren't as clear cut or straightforward – with these groups, they tell you exactly how to be included and stick to it.

But if you are not a member of a gang, or you don't think the cult life is for you, then you are stuck in the sticky hot mess of the rest of society, where everyone has different ideas of what are the right and wrong ways to live, everyone sounds totally plausible that their way is the only right way and you spend your whole life being guided and controlled through fear of exclusion by using a highly effective method – that of guilt. By not following a rule, you are told you are less than, that you are somehow not worthy of inclusion and therefore need to get back into line.  It's your problem if you can't quite decide which rule is the one you are supposed to follow.

When I look back at my childhood years, I didn't feel like I fitted in the way other kids did.  There were lots of reasons why maybe I should have - I was into Star Wars, superheroes, cartoons and Top of the Pops.  But I also loved reading and escaping into a world that was completely detached from my own, set in the days of Jane Austen, Charlotte Bronte, even Shakespeare.  And I loved facts and trivia.  I loved knowledge and learning.  I loved it and I was good at it.  The majority of the children around me liked bits of who I was, but not the whole.  I wasn't sure if partly fitting in wasn't worse than not fitting in at all.

Eventually, I was coming top of the class so consistently that, well, it became expected. It was expected that I would pass my GCSEs, pass my A-Levels, go to university, get a good degree – and I did all of that, just as was expected.  It was expected that I would get a good job and that my abilities and skills would be valued and nurtured, and I would fulfil my end of the bargain by following the rules and continuing to work hard.  As far as I knew, I was following all of the rules as I was supposed to and hoped that it was now going to start paying off.

But at work I hit a new set of rules – adult rules that differed from teacher rules – and I realised fairly quickly that, in workplaces, colleagues and managers don't see someone to be admired for how much they know or how fast they pick skills up - they see a threat.

The very things that had been expected of me while growing up now made my first steps into employment extremely uncomfortable. Nobody was impressed by my qualifications or my test scores – in fact, they only seemed to antagonize them.  I thought that there was some way that I could impress, by being smarter, more committed to my job, do more hours, work harder - then they would see what an asset I am, then they would see *me*.  I didn't realise until I was sitting in the doctor's office that day, having fallen apart so completely, that the harder I tried to become what they wanted me to be, the more rules I tried to follow, even when they were clearly in conflict, the more the pressure to comply built inside me until my brain just couldn't function any more.

So how do you balance between others' expectations and your own desires? How do you make the right choices for your life when you may have been conditioned to keep other people happy?

You need social connection, but you need it on your own terms, otherwise you fall into the trap of becoming someone that you don't recognize. What I'm attempting to do in this book is provide you with the tools you need to be able to identify when guilt is coming up for you – to learn how to recognize it, and how to analyse it to find out where it is coming from. Then, once you know it's there, how do you get rid of it? I'm going to give you some tips on how to reframe situations to retain control and therefore your own perspective, making it more difficult for guilt to take hold.

I'm going to walk you through how to live your life guilt free from this day on. How to manage your choices, decisions, energy, relationships and your time so that every day you go to bed knowing that you had the best day for you possible.

And finally, I want you to think bigger than happy – I want you to live with passion and joy and loving your life every single day, and so we are going to be looking at ways that you can live with passion, taking your life to the next level without the weight of uncertainty fear and guilt dragging you back.

But who am I to take you through this? I have no formal qualifications in psychology or neuropsychology. I haven't studied the human brain in laboratories for years. But I *have* studied human beings, both in my personal life and with my clients. I have experienced my own guilt and watched others experience theirs. I have lived in the shadow of guilt and have found a way that helped me through – and helped those who trusted me to come with them on their own path. If I can help just one person to live with less guilt, I will have made a difference.

It makes me so angry to see truly beautiful people torn apart by the rule book that they have been trying to follow. I see it as my mission to show you that the power to change expectations and release yourself from the guilt of trying to please others has always been with you, if you take the time to look.

So – are you ready for your journey through the guilt trip?

## 2: Guilt Is Good – Said Nobody Ever (Except Me)

As a human being, you have to balance your physical, mental and emotional wellbeing in order to survive. You have to stay physically healthy, mentally stimulated and maintain emotional stability and safety. An imbalance in these can create stress or overwhelm, even disease or injury, but it is probably the case that you prefer focusing on one more than the others. A lot will depend on which one feel easiest to focus on, which one feels the hardest to deal with or which one feels the most important to you at any given time. And let's be honest, the trickiest one to feel okay about is your emotional security.

Your physical wellbeing seems to be the most understood of the three – you know how the body works at a biological level, you know what to put in it, what comes out of it and logically, you know the 'right' things to do. Ah, if it was only that easy, eh?

You know the right conditions for your physical body but without focusing on the mental and emotional elements as well, this can seem the hardest one to get right. Comfort eating happens when you use a physical sensation – that of being full of sugar, or salt, or fat, or whatever is your numbing food of choice – to overcome an emotional response that you don't want to feel or acknowledge. This is particularly odd when you think that most comfort eating will lead you to feel emotionally even more out of control and can send you spiralling down into self-doubt, guilt and shame. Because you know the right things to do you, by default, know the wrong things to do as well, and when emotions get uncomfortable or painful, it is a simple solution to make your body pay for your emotional pain.

19

As with the physical body, the brain can seem quite sensible and straightforward, looking like a simple logical machine, a biological computer designed to help you think rationally and make good considered decisions. And so it is. But you know that many of your decisions are not made logically or rationally. In fact, it can sometimes feel that your brain goes out of its way to complicate things, allowing you to go off on tangents of random thoughts that have nothing to do with what you are doing right now and can slow you down or make you stop completely. Overthinking can be as dangerous to your wellbeing as overeating, by making you focus on the elephants in the room that are just not there.

How many times have you had to make a really important decision, and felt stifled with too many options, opinions, perspectives, and possibilities? It can feel like your brain is sabotaging all of your efforts to think clearly, by bringing up some rubbish that you did at school twenty years ago, or to remind you of that ex-partner who always said you would never amount to much, or to tell you that you can't possibly feel able to make that decision without consulting every person in your Pilates WhatsApp group.

This is because even when the brain is trying its hardest to think objectively, it is constantly at the mercy of your emotions and they are not logical at all – they are a stewing pot of all sorts of concoctions, most of which you don't want to admit are even there. As much as your brain likes rational thoughts and streams of consciousness that are easy to follow and analyse, it is forced to filter everything through this emotional stew, having each objective thought wrapped in a subjective emotion that can radically change how you think from that moment on.

Take, for example, buying a pair of shoes. You know the ones that you like, because you saw your friend wearing them at the party last week, and as soon as you saw them, you pictured every outfit you have that would look amazing with them. Logically, you could now make the decision to get the shoes, right? *I want the shoes + the shoes are available = new pair of shoes and happy me.*

But … at the same party last week, a mutual friend told you that they had gone for a drink with this friend, who, after a few drinks, had told them that she felt that you were stalking her, trying to be like her in your gestures, what you say and what you do (hey, I never said it was a friend that you liked). This is going to make you feel both angry as hell and hurt, thinking that someone has such a low and quite frankly outrageous opinion of you. So now, wearing those shoes brings up far different emotions and the chances of you ever getting those shoes have just gone quicker than that friend's number got deleted from your phone.

How you treat your body, and how you manage your mental wellbeing are both intimately connected with the emotions that you feel. And as a special treat, you can't even choose what emotions you experience. It would be fantastic if you could list out every emotion you could ever have, and take a few off the menu, but they don't work that way. Your emotional responses are an on / off switch – you either feel or you don't. And if you feel, you feel *everything*. No picking and choosing only to feel good – to experience the good you *have* to be prepared to experience the bad. And for some people that is not a decision that can be made easily, if at all.

When the doctor gave me anti-depressants to stop my suicidal thoughts, it was a relief for a while not to feel, but it soon became more uncomfortable than ever. The lack of feeling anything started to affect my link to my own self-identity. When I looked in the mirror, I wasn't really sure of the person staring back. I didn't feel I knew her at all, or if I did, I only knew her as someone I had vaguely heard of. Who was she? What made her tick?

I had always been a huge fan of stand-up comedy and it has always been my go-to when I feel down or need a quick reminder that there is a way to make people laugh. While I was on the antidepressants, however, I just couldn't see what was so funny about any of it. I would put on DVDs of gigs that would usually have had me in tears of laughter, stomach muscles aching from not being able to stop laughing. Not only did I not laugh, but my brain actually couldn't work out *how* it could possibly be funny. Why on earth would you laugh at something so illogical, silly, nonsensical?

Without the input of the emotions, my brain looked at it as almost a logic problem, an interesting puzzle to be solved. I could break down the elements of what made it funny, but I would not have been able to make myself laugh over it. I could put together the formula of a joke, but it was missing the special sauce provided by the emotional context that is the essence of why different people laugh at different jokes.

I understood why it was necessary to turn off my emotions for a while, given the stage I had reached, but it was not long before I was working with my doctor to get me off the medication, and I swore from that day on that I would pay more attention to my emotional wellbeing so I never had to turn them off again. It turned off a core, essential part of who I was and the part I played in the world. If you cannot feel emotions appropriately, it is nearly impossible to connect with others on a meaningful level. It is why those suffering with depression or anxiety have the unenviable daily challenge of feeling nothing or feeling too much, a trial that none of us ever want to face and why they deserve nothing but our utmost respect and compassion.

You have to feel the full range of emotions in order to experience the ones you want to, such as joy, happiness or love. But what do you do with those emotions that you don't want – things such as anger, hurt, sadness, pain, or guilt?

Even though you have to experience all of them or none of them, you still try to sort the emotions you have into two logical, rational groups that may help you avoid at least the full intensity of those more uncomfortable ones. You divide them up into 'good' and 'bad' emotions and try to deal with them in different ways. This idea that certain emotions are better than others, and that you a) get to define which is which and b) get to then deal with them all differently, is unhelpful and just plain wrong. This misrepresents what your emotions are actually for.

All emotions are generated as a response to your current or present situation – emotion doesn't exist anywhere but in the present moment. Now, you might say, ah, but I feel pain, or hurt, or happiness from past events. No, you don't. You're not using your memory to recall and access the past emotion – you are remembering the event and then the brain is remembering which emotion that evoked at the time, and it evokes it again. The emotion is recreated fresh each time you have that memory.

This is why things such as NLP, Neuro Linguistic Programming, are so effective – it reprograms the brain to bring forward a different emotion to a past event, to help you process it more effectively. Emotions are just a response to the stimulus in front of you, whatever that is. They are designed to keep you alive (thank you, survival instinct) by making you respond and react to that situation in a helpful way.

And you're happy to recognize and acknowledge the emotions you can cope with and what it is trying to tell you – if you feel happy, you smile, if you are excited, you cheer, if you are confused, you ask more questions, seek more answers. These may be the ones that you class as good or positive emotions, because they seem to take you forward and make your journey lighter.

The problem comes when the emotion brought up does not make you respond in a helpful way and in fact can make things worse. When this happens, you view them as bad or negative emotions, immediately separating them from the more obvious 'positive' ones and framing them immediately as problems that you need to eradicate.

Yet even the emotions that feel the most destructive, such as anger or guilt, can be a positive impact on your life, if you pay attention to them closely. In reality, they are no different to any of the other more empowering emotions – they are trying to get you to react in a certain way. If you feel guilty, for example, it can be making you feel that your actions are not in line with your core values and it is that fact that makes it very uncomfortable and unpleasant.

What this means is that you can't take it for granted that an emotion has only one meaning or that there is only one way of responding. You need to unpack the emotion and the reasons behind it to really know whether you should pay attention to it or not. When you look specifically at guilt this is even more necessary – because it feels so unpleasant, it can be easy to just want to dismiss it as soon as possible.

It may even be that you are reading this book because you don't want to feel guilty any more. What I'm saying is – hold that thought for the remainder of this book, because I truly believe there are certain contexts in which feeling guilty is actually something to be hopeful about, as it shows you the best version of yourself (you are just not living up to it right now).

What I'm saying is this – that in order to be a healthy, well-balanced human being, you have to be able to balance the needs of your physical, mental and emotional security and health together, and to do so it is essential that no emotions are silenced. All must be acknowledged because they are trying to tell you something. However, any one of those emotions can have good and bad aspects to them – each one can influence the way you make your choices in life, and it is not always a positive contribution to help you make the best decision for you. It is that difference that the next part of this book focuses on.

As much as I say that guilt can be good, I know also it can be very destructive and damaging to your happiness and wellbeing. I believe that there are two very different sides to guilt and being able to tell the difference between them is critical to you finding true joy. One can help you reach a level of potential that you never thought possible; the other will do all it can to keep you small. Don't let it. Walk through it with me now, so you too can tell the difference between guilt that makes you move, and guilt that makes you glued.

## 3:  Guilt That Moves and Guilt That Glues

I t might not be a popular belief, but I genuinely believe that guilt can be one of the most positive emotions that you have.  The problem isn't in the emotion itself – it is usually in the reason behind it.  As we already covered, emotion inspires you to respond in certain ways, but it is wrong to think that this means that an emotion can only evoke one type of response.

It sounds logical to think of one emotion, one reaction – when you're happy, you laugh; when you're sad, you cry.  But if you break that down a bit, you will find that it is not that straightforward.  When you're happy, you laugh – but you can also sing, smile, hum, dance, hug, run, breathe – the list is endless.  It all boils down to the same emotion – that you are happy. But how you show that happiness will depend on your personality, as well as the context and the reason for feeling happy.  You may feel happy in the supermarket, but you wouldn't necessarily go singing and dancing down the aisles.  In fact, scrap that – I recommend you absolutely sing and dance down the aisles – and try to get others to join in.

But think of when you are feeling sad – yes you cry, but you might also go very quiet, you might isolate yourself from others, you might put on sad music, or watch a sad movie, or you might hug, or run or breathe. Sometimes the actions themselves can't tell you what mood someone is in – but likewise you can't predict exactly what actions or responses they will give to show their emotion either.  The only thing you can use to gauge the emotion you or others are feeling is to look at the context (i.e. what is happening right now, what is the situation you are facing) and the reason (i.e. what has triggered you into feeling that way).

Guilt is no different. While it may feel that you experience guilt in the same way every time, it is by checking the context and the reason that you can work out if the guilt is positive and empowering, or destructive. I call it the two sides of guilt: Guilt That Moves You or Guilt That Glues You.

## Guilt That Moves You

Picture the scene. You've just got in from a day at work and it's fair to say it wasn't a good one. Stressed and tired, you just want to eat dinner, go for a long soak in the bath and pretend to forget that you have to go back in tomorrow morning. Just as you lay in the foamy water, your eyes fluttering shut as you have a well-deserved nap, your phone rings and doorbell rings, and a friend announces that they are standing outside your front door with a bottle of wine, ready to offload all of their stresses onto you. To say you are irritated is something of an understatement. It's not that you don't like your friend, or even that you wouldn't like a glass or two of wine and a general moan about your day. But that water is so good ... and your aching muscles are appreciating the heat. You, still half asleep and fully stressed, do not have the capacity to think of diplomacy, manners, or compromises – you just want to hide under the bubbles. So, you make a snappy comment about turning up unannounced, and they apologise and hang up. You hear their car rev into action and as they drive away, you slide back down in the water, but the moment is ruined. You've fully woken up and you stub your toe on the hot water tap. Definitely time for bed. Waking up in the morning, refreshed and ready to face a new day, you suddenly remember how you spoke to your friend, and you flush red with embarrassment and feel guilty that you sent them away in such a way.

Guilt such as this can feel really uncomfortable, but how long you sit in that discomfort is dependent on what kind of guilt it is. Guilt can be so uncomfortable that you are unable to think of anything else until you have addressed it. Emotions are deliberately difficult to ignore, because they are part of our survival system, but it doesn't stop you from trying.

In fact, some wellness businesses are based on telling you that you can free yourself from negative emotions with various techniques and ideologies. And I will say, many of them can. There are some extremely effective therapies that can help you reduce anxiety-inducing emotions and for many, they work brilliantly. But for me, this is treating the symptom, not the cause. If you feel an emotion and you don't get to the bottom of what is causing it, then any treatments, therapies or practices you follow are only ever going to scratch the itch, but not release you from it completely.

I'm going to take it that, as you are reading this book, you want a more permanent solution. And the trick to that lies in answering one simple question:

**What do I feel I need to do next?**

Once you know the answer to this, you can then delve deeper into the context and the reasons for the guilt – but neither of those will make any sense unless you ask this first.

How would you answer this question? It might sound basic, but you would be surprised how many times you feel guilty, and anxiety starts kicking in because you can't actually think of what you should do next. Look back at the failed bath night, and picture yourself in that situation. If I asked you, what do you feel you need to do next – how do you think you would answer? Do you have an immediate answer? Does it take you a few minutes, but then you work it out? Or are you drawing blanks?

The heart of answering this question lies in tapping into your own core values and beliefs. Everything that you do gets filtered through your own code of ethics, your own moral code, or your core belief system. This code or system reminds you who you are and who you want to be. It holds your view of what your personality and character are, and what behaviour you expect from yourself.

Any time you take action, it gets filtered through that code and you get a sense of whether the action is in line with your moral code or not. If everything is aligned, then you get to experience a range of appropriate emotions in response to the action. But if there is a mismatch between your code and the action you have taken, guilt is triggered.

Here, guilt is acting as an early warning system that tells you – *hold up, something is wrong*. What you are saying or doing is not who you are or who you want to be.  And because of that misalignment, guilt will remain at the centre of your attention – it is the big flashing red light or the loud alarm siren in your mind that everything is **not** okay.  In the example, this is waking up the next morning and remembering the phone call.  This sets off the alarm, and you now need to deal with it.  And usually that means taking action.

**Guilt that moves you** refers to that feeling you get when, upon reflection, you absolutely know that you need to do something to correct the course your life is taking.  There is no option to ignore it - no amount of stuffing your face with junk food, drinking yourself into oblivion, or hiding away in your dressing gown binge watching box sets, is going to make you feel better, or ease the situation.  In fact, the avoidance that such actions would give take you even further away from resolving the problem.

And you know this.  It may feel like a logical decision, but it is driven by a far more compulsive need that needs you to look and act like the person you know you are.  There may be people who give you advice to just leave it, let it go, but you will know without question that you must do something.  And … you normally know what it is you need to do.  Sometimes it is an apology and an explanation.  Sometimes it is paying back money, making financial amends, or giving some of your time up to show them that they matter to you.  Whatever it is, you will feel compelled to do it, and no matter how uncomfortable or awkward it is, you know that you will ultimately feel better because your actions are back in line with your core beliefs and values.

In the example above, you may have shaky hands while you call your friend to explain and apologise, or to invite them over the following evening, preparing yourself for them to ignore the call or slam the phone down on you.  But you will still call.  And you will keep trying until you feel that you have made amends.  The alarm bells will not stop ringing until you feel that you have done everything that you possibly could.

This is why I say guilt can be good – it's good because it reminds you of who you are at a deep emotional level, of the type of person you are and want to be, and it lets you know when you are not running true to that.  Even better, it makes you feel extremely uncomfortable until you have sorted out exactly what you are going to do to make you feel better. The discomfort is such that you are compelled to change your behaviour and correct your course, in order to feel more aligned. Working well then, guilt is a great tool for keeping true and honest with yourself. You recognize the feeling, review what you have just done, and assess how you feel about that. If it is out of line with what you think is authentic to you, you will take action – you may apologise for not being tactful or gentle, you might revisit a conversation that ended badly, maybe phone back that person you just left to go to voicemail. You will feel compelled to act if it is not in line with who you think you are and if guilt is working well, you welcome that response.

If you feel this need to act, then your guilt is moving you towards action – it is giving you no choice but to realign yourself. When you ask yourself 'what do I feel I need to do next', and you feel compelled to do something AND you know what it is you want to do, then your guilt is positive and empowering – it is reminding you that you can be better, that you *can* be the person you want to be.

Guilt is not an emotion that you necessarily want to invite into your life too often – you are hopefully also learning how to avoid similar situations in the future – but if you feel like this, then it is an opportunity for you to adjust your course, to change lanes and getting back to be the best version of yourself.

Once you recognise that the guilt you're feeling is making you want to move, you can look into the context of the situation and the reasons it happened and can begin to piece together what action you will want to take. In the bath situation, the context would be that you had a stressful day, that had caused you to feel more anxious and tired than usual. The reason for your outburst, therefore, was that you were trying to make yourself feel better by running the bath and giving yourself some very necessary self-care, and the disappointment of having that time interrupted made you irritated. You felt that there is never enough time or priority given to your needs and taking care of you. All of that culminated in being snappy to your friend.

Notice that neither the context nor the reason *excuses* or *justifies* your behaviour – at the end of the day, you messed up and you now have to put in some effort to repair the friendship which may mean an awkward conversation. This may also involve you being told that it wasn't a justified response. But knowing these details does at least give you a better understanding of what happened and therefore you can then choose how much to explain to your friend and how much they may need to know in order for you to feel that you have realigned with your core values.   Once you know that you need to do something, the context and the reason can help you work out what that something is.

## Guilt That Glues You

It is often the case that you ask yourself, '*what do I feel I need to do next*' and you draw a blank.  This is natural – if you think about some of the words used in connection with guilt – '*awash with guilt*', '*guilt swept over me*' – you have to acknowledge that the intensity of that emotion may be so great that you can't think straight.  This is usually because guilt also sweeps in other debilitating emotions such as embarrassment, shame, anger, frustration, pain and sadness.  It can whip all other emotions up so much that sometimes, you can barely breathe and so it can be normal to feel that your brain can't process anything, and you are unable to think straight or take any action.

Even if this happens though, there usually comes a point where those emotions are not helping the situation and your brain comes through the emotional fog and tries to solve the problem, to help it out of feeling such a mass of different emotions.  When you're talking about the guilt that moves you, this is the point where you shake your head, blow your nose, dry your eyes and start to think of what to do – you ask the question.  But there are occasions that even when you get to that point, the answers are still not there, and you still don't know what to do.  And this inability to move on and solve it can be excruciatingly painful and bewildering.

Why would this be the case?

First things first, there is a fundamental difference here between not *wanting* to act and not knowing *how* to act.  With the guilt that moves you, the solution that you know would resolve the situation may feel impossible to put into action.  The right action may involve the breakup of a relationship, deciding to quit work, or moving your home, and these are such huge decisions that you will defer the action to take for a long time, maybe even years.  But it won't stop you feeling that compulsion to act.  That little voice in your head and your heart that is telling you that it needs to be done.  And there really is only so long you can avoid it until the impact on the quality of your life is so bad that you can't get away with it any more.  That would still count as the guilt that moves you, even though you are choosing not to go along with it for however long you possibly can.

But what about when you feel guilty, but don't really know why.  When you get that gnawing ball in your stomach that you are doing something wrong, that others will judge you for getting it wrong, that you will be criticized, laughed at, ignored or exposed – yet you can't trace the reason why?  You can't see what action is causing the guilt, so you can't correct course.

Not knowing how to act is the result of guilt that glues you.  This is where you genuinely have no idea what to do.  There are no possibilities that you are avoiding, no options that you pretend to ignore – you are quite literally drawing a complete blank.  You feel helpless, confused and lost, because you feel that you have done something wrong, but you can't piece the clues together to help you know your next best action.  The reason for this:  the guilt you are feeling is triggered by a code of ethics, morality or core values that are not yours to begin with.

That can be difficult to understand or recognize – if you have hurt or upset someone, surely that goes against your core values?  That is true - there may be components of what you did that are not in line with the way you want to act.  But the reason you can't think of the best way to resolve it is because the guilt is not something that comes from within yourself but from an external source.

Family, friends, bosses, magazines, celebrities, social media – these influence your self-identity and your behaviour and sometimes drive you towards actions that are not what you want to do.  It is almost always the case that these external influences have no idea that they are having such an effect on you, but it doesn't stop it being true.  A mother complaining that she is overweight will influence body image.  A school teacher who rewards the 'good' children will influence intellectual confidence.  The social media posts showing a perfect lifestyle that doesn't look remotely like your own will influence opinions of success.

While they may not be doing it deliberately, these others are giving you a view of what they consider to be right or wrong behaviour. And these views then filter into your own thoughts and you start to be unable to tell the difference between what you feel for yourself and what has been embedded by others.

You may feel like you want to rebel against the idea that others can have exert such control over you, but it is so subtle that you may not even see it as control until you are in the throes of guilt. Because the rule that is being broken was not yours to begin with, you don't understand where it comes from and you can't rationalize or define it in any way. When you 'break' it, you are unable to know the next move, instead having to wait for others to provide you with it, or at least an idea of what it might be. You are glued to the spot, trapped in the feelings of guilt and discomfort, until someone helps you get out.

Because so many of these values and rules are implied and intangible, there is no one who comes to your rescue, and so you are left feeling that you are in an impossible situation that cannot be fixed. From there, you start assuming that the problem is no longer the situation, or someone else's opinion – the problem is *you*.

It might seem to be hopeless, but once you know that this is where you are, it becomes easier to then work out where it does come from and therefore what to do with it. Go back again to the context and the reason for the situation you find yourself in. What are the circumstances that created the situation? And in that context, what created your response to it? It's in answering these questions that you can really identify where the guilt is coming from.

Look at the context of the bath situation above – if the guilt of being frustrated with your unexpected visitor wasn't truly from you, it might be that there was additional context. Maybe there was a previous occasion when you had genuinely been out, but that person had told all of your mutual friends that you deliberately avoided them, which made your friends challenge you and get you to explain yourself.

In this case, the embarrassment and guilt you feel may be more connected to your worry about what others will think or say, rather than upsetting that person. In fact, if they have put you in this position in the past, you may not really be super excited about seeing them anyway – you may worry that they will find something else wrong with your behaviour that they then tell others about!

But it feels like a catch 22 situation – if you don't apologise, then the likelihood of them criticising you to your friends goes up, but if you do apologise, they may still feel able to tell others and your name is mud anyway. Given that your main worry is what your friends will hear or think, each option you think of is not about whether it addresses the issue, but rather how it will be received by the others who should not really be involved at all.

When you feel that you cannot move, and you begin to explore the context and reason behind it, you may realise that a lot of the thoughts you were having, and a lot of the rationale, wasn't created by going deep within you, to your own core values. They may have been created by you hearing or picturing particular individuals and their opinions or responses to your actions. If, the morning after, rather than feeling bad that you hurt someone's feeling, you immediately pictured the reactions your friends would be giving to the texts that were almost certainly heading to them – this is external guilt provided by others.

This can be hard to get your head around but is the key to being able to shirk off guilt trips and make decisions on your own. When you feel guilty because of values that others are putting onto you, you don't make good decisions for yourself. Instead, you surrender your decision making and power to others, and therefore have to wait for them to tell you what to do next. If someone has been particularly irritating you, you may already know that the friendship is probably on its end run anyway. While you don't want to upset anyone, you may feel that what others want you to do is not what you would do if the choice was solely yours. In this case, it isn't. The expectations from others over what you will do can override your own choices to the point where you may act with no personal will at all – you'll do it because they will think it is the right thing to do.

But there is a problem with this, and it boils down to the universal laws of guilt trips:

1. *Everyone will have an opinion on what you are doing and whether it is right or wrong.*
2. *Every opinion will be different and probably complete opposites.*

And here lies the problem when you have guilt that glues you. You are stuck and have to wait for someone else to tell you the next thing to do – but you can guarantee that more than one person will give you an opinion and you can almost guarantee that each person will contradict and contrast with each other. And you will be stuck even more – you need advice from others but none of them agree! If you couldn't decide on the next best thing to do before, you definitely won't be able to when everyone else gets involved.

This is why the guilt that glues you can be so destructive. You can't move out of guilt if you don't know the right solution – and you have given away your power to decide by being more concerned with what others think than what is right for you. The longer you are unable to take corrective action, the more risk there is that you will start to believe that you *can't* get out of it, and that is when you open yourself up to lower self-confidence, lower self-worth and increased self-doubt, creating a vicious cycle of disempowerment that continues to tell you that you are not good enough until you believe it to be true.

In chapter 7, there is a chance to go into more detail about how to recognize where this guilt is coming from and what to do about it. The trick is to identify where you have given your power away, who you have given it to and reframe that connection so that you take back control.

For now, think back on some of the occasions you have felt guilty and ask the question - *What do I feel I needed to do next?* Can you feel that urge to correct course, or did you feel stuck and out of ideas? The key to living guilt free is not in eradicating guilt completely, but rather to know the difference between the two types. You can then focus on paying attention to the guilt that moves you, as it encourages you to be the best you. You can also deal with the guilt that glues you by identifying who you have given power to and how to get it back. This is the first step to living guilt free.

# 4:  What Are the Effects of Guilt?

I get a real assortment of reactions when I talk about my work with guilt.  Some people I speak to are genuinely interested in the subject, curious to know more.  Others are ready to give me a whole list of why they feel guilty - sometimes even telling me that they feel guilty for giving me their list.  Sometimes I have people feign disinterest, disengaging from further discussion although I can usually spot them half listening when I am talking to someone else.  And finally, I have the people who feel that it is not only enough for me to not talk about guilt with them, but I shouldn't talk about it with anyone.

And I get it.  Guilt is a really uncomfortable emotion to sit with and as discussed before, it is supposed to be.  If it was easy to feel, then it wouldn't spur you on to take corrective action or to change your behaviour.  But everyone has a slightly different tolerance level for how much they can cope with and this then creates the variety of reactions I have when I mention my subject matter.

You are used to experiencing a range of emotions at any one time, but you will know that there always seems to be one that rises above the rest.  If someone asked you at any point how you were feeling, you would immediately recognise the predominant one, but then it would take a while longer for you to separate that out from the others bubbling below the surface.

Guilt is no different and in fact, it does an impressive job of suffocating all of the other emotions.  It acts as a blanket, meaning that all other emotions have to go through this blanket, this filter, in order to be felt.

Take for example, a time when you felt really happy.  For some, happiness feels intangible and temporary, and a mood that can be changed instantly and dramatically by the wrong look, or the wrong turn of phrase or response. And this is true of many other emotions – they are transient and flighty, and you remain aware that your emotions and mood could change very quickly. It feels like you could blink, and you would miss it.

Then think of a time you felt guilty. It is a difficult emotion to shake off – even after you have redressed the issue. It lies heavy upon you, weighing you down for quite a while before you finally begin to remember what life was like before the guilt arrived. And that is if you manage to address the guilt at all. If you are unable to resolve it, then it starts to affect every other feeling you have. There will be times when you still experience the other emotions, but you will be aware that it is through a filter of guilt.

Imagine winning the lottery and feeling incredibly happy to have won, but also guilty that there are others less fortunate than yourself that were not so lucky. You may still feel happy, but you may also feel unentitled to spend so freely while others around you continue to struggle.

You are constantly trying to knock guilt away from your conscious thoughts, and if you let your guard down, it will suddenly flood your system. Everything feels just a little bit off and uncomfortable which is why I completely understand the responses I get. Depending on how long you have lived with the guilt, and what other emotions you are trying to experience, you may want to avoid any mention of guilt because you think that by ignoring it you can somehow make it go away.

Unfortunately, because guilt is so closely tied with your core values and beliefs and is felt in a similar way to your survival instinct, it is impossible to ignore or lessen its impact. Like your physical response to fire, which is to get away from it as quickly as possible, guilt impresses upon you that something is not right and will continue to feel urgent until it is resolved. Ignoring it will only make it feel more intense as it tries to constantly drag back your attention to the issue. And the methods it uses to retain your focus impacts every aspect of you – your physical body, your conscious and subconscious mind and your emotions.

When you are struggling with guilt, everything gets affected and because of this it can be difficult to identify it as guilt - it can seem easier to call it by another name so that it feels more comfortable. But the first step to dealing with guilt and learning to let it go is to be able to see it for what it is, and that means understanding how it is likely to affect you.

You may find that many of the things I describe can also be attributed to other emotions – and that is true. As you now know, each emotion can trigger a number of different but similar reactions, so I am not saying that if you have these effects happening to you, that you are definitely struggling with guilt. But I will say that these are the effects I have seen through my work with my clients and have become fairly good indicators for me that there is some guilt that needs to be identified and addressed. Once you can see guilt for what it is, you can overcome it and deal with it effectively.

## Physical Effects

Because the urgency of guilt seems to mimic the survival instincts you have, many of the physical effects are similar to your flight or fight response. This makes sense, if you consider the discomfort you experience when you feel guilty about something. It is usually so intense that you feel that you need to do something, whether that is trying to run away or to tackle it head on.

This is intimately tied to the type of guilt you have. As a reminder, if you have the internal guilt that requires you to move and get back in line with your core values and beliefs, then you are likely to strike out, to take massive action to try to overcome the guilt, over apologising or over-compensating for your previous actions and potentially creating even more problems. If the guilt originates from someone or something else externally, then you are likely to feel stuck, like the rabbit in the headlights and unable to decide what is the right next step.

With positive guilt your actions will change the situation in some way and create a different dynamic (hopefully a more positive one). This allows you to recognise that there is no longer a stressful situation and you climb down from that fight or flight reaction.

37

With negative guilt you are unable to move from the pain and guilt that you are facing, and so the feeling of helplessness and loss of direction festers and grows ever deeper and more damaging.

The lack of ideas does not cancel out the stress and the flight response that you will have, and so you stay at high levels of stress, and you don't know how to get out of it. It is no wonder then that many people experiencing acute guilt also have significant anxiety or even panic attacks.

Both anxiety and panic attacks are signs from your body that it needs to be doing something and that it is preparing itself for action, but without the mind providing it with any sense of direction, that stress has nowhere to go. This is made even worse when you consider that, to get rid of the guilt, you have to acknowledge it and work through it and if your stress levels are already very high, that is literally the last thing you will feel able to cope with.

With physical 'injuries', the healing comes from cleaning out the wound and you know that the temporary extra pain will be worth it in the end. When it comes to your mental wellbeing, however, you are not at all sure that the ability to heal is there, and so you fear taking on the additional pain because you are not confident that the damage won't be permanent. Without facing the guilt, you then force all of the stress back into your body and find that you are more prone to anxiety, panic attacks or insomnia.

It can be exhausting to feel like this all of the time, which explains why people who are suffering from unacknowledged guilt may turn to substances such as alcohol and drugs or will binge on food (whether in quantity or quality of food) to try to get rid of the discomfort. Guilt can have the same persistence as a mosquito bite – even the best creams in the world cannot get rid of the itching completely and so you have to distract yourself while your body fights it. With guilt, because it is an emotional 'bite', it will continue to itch for as long as the cause of the guilt gets ignored. And no amount of creams or distractions are going to ease the itch – the danger is that you use increasingly more distractions and end up doing some real physical harm to yourself.

If you are experiencing anxiety, or panic attacks, you may find that the underlying issue is guilt over your situation, or your circumstances or that of others, and it feels impossible to resolve. Thinking that something is impossible leads to the feelings of helplessness, and hopelessness, with the danger that it feels so insurmountable that you stop trying.

## Mental Effects

As you can see, a lot of the physical effects are symptomatic or caused by the mind trying to process the guilt. You have to remember that your brain will always try to protect you both physically and mentally and so the first thing it will try to do is to find reasons and excuses to discharge the guilt as quickly as possible. You may try to pin responsibility onto someone else, or you might blame your upbringing, your childhood or violent treatment you received from partners on the guilt that you are feeling. In order to keep you mentally safe, your mind pushes the ownership of the guilt away from you, creating distance between you and it. However, as with the physical effects, without being dealt with, the guilt will remain, even when far away, and your mind can never fully move onto the next thing as it is keeping an eye on the guilt to make sure it doesn't make another appearance.

The strain of having to constantly factor in guilt takes its toll, and this could trigger a couple of different responses:

You could ease into it, admit that you need to deal with the guilt, and begin to process it. If it is internal guilt that moves you, then this process will be quite positive, and you may even wonder why it took you so long to open up to it. There is a lightness in feeling back in control, even when the actions you need to take to resolve it are uncomfortable.

But if it is externally created guilt, where you will not know your next best move, then your mind is not provided with an escape route that solves the problem, so it moves on to trying to minimise the damage by pushing responsibility onto others. Unfortunately, in many cases it actually makes it worse.

Sometimes you face guilt that you can't reconcile by changing your direction, so instead you go to the other end of the scale, rebelling entirely against the 'wrong' that you believe that you have committed and doing as close to the exact opposite as possible. In this case, the smoker doesn't smoke one cigarette, but the whole pack; the drinker doesn't take a glass, they take the bottle; one slice of cake becomes the whole cake stand.

Once you believe that you have guilt that you cannot correct, the only alternative option might be to go all in. You are trying to regain control of the situation, to provide yourself with a rationale that provides protection against the guilt, but you know it is short term – once the moment is over, and the cigarettes, drink or cake are gone – the guilt will come back with even more ferocity, ever more potency and the destructive cycle starts again. This time however, there is even more evidence that the guilt is valid and so it becomes less of a cycle and more of a spiral.

This need to rebel can be tied into the 'fight' physical response you have when you try to get away from the discomfort of guilt. Both are focused on taking action and doing something in order to get rid of the emotions. But action requires effort and does not bode well as a long-term strategy. Eventually you will get tired and run out of fight. This is when your mind can stop fighting and instead ease into acceptance, not just of the guilt but what it says about the kind of person you are.

Feeling guilty about your actions can quickly lead you to question the type of person you are or are capable of being. It convinces you that there is a standard of behaviour that you are not reaching and given enough time, you will start to question whether you are capable of ever getting there. As with the smoker who gives up trying to quit and instead smokes more, it is possible to get to the point where you convince yourself that you are just not up to the challenge and you stop trying to meet it.

Your self-worth is tied to your ability to match your aspirational moral codes, and therefore not meeting them begins to convince you that you are not worth as much as you thought you were. And when you get tired from trying to keep pushing the guilt away, you begin to question your ability to push any more, to achieve anything different than what you have got now, and so your confidence also takes a considerable hit.

If you don't feel that you can make the required change, and you don't feel that you are worthy enough of the change anyway – you won't make the change.  You therefore stay in the guilt even longer, doubting yourself more each day, and feeling more and more trapped.

## Emotional Effects

While the physical effects are the result of the increased mental and emotional stress (and your inability to think of a way out of the fight or flight response), the mental and emotional effects generate that stress, but in slightly different ways.

The mental processes you go through focus on the discharge of the guilt and pain through rationalisation and justification and the stress increases as those arguments fail to work.  As it becomes more difficult for you to rationalise and justify, you trigger emotions that are intended to discharge the discomfort instead.  Emotions provide the energy, the charge, behind the discharge – for example, frustration at not being able to get rid of the guilt eventually gets replaced by anger, directed at others but essentially powered by the frustration that you're feeling over a situation that you do not feel that you can control.

In fact, anger is one of the go-to emotions when feeling guilt – it allows you to blast at someone, which has a lot of energy behind it and therefore discharges a lot of the pain and discomfort.  Also, the typical response from others when you are angry is to leave you alone and, in that moment, that might be preferable to them finding out about the guilt you feel.  When you consider 'gaslighting' – the practice of manipulating the perspective of another person in order to make them question their own reality – it is typically associated with displays of anger.  And that makes sense – if I wanted to stop you seeing the truth in my guilt, I could distract you through anger, but it is more effective to make you question your version of events to the point where you are not even sure that the guilt ever existed. The anger displayed as outrage covers the manipulation and as the perpetrator, it buys me time to find a way of avoiding feeling guilty.

I have spoken with clients coming out of abusive relationships, where their partner did exactly this – showed righteous anger at their honesty being questioned but incorporated a degree of doubt in my clients' account of what happened so that the focus came off them and onto my clients who were left wondering if they were in fact the ones that were wrong.

In my clients' case, it was clear that it was an intentionally aggressive act, but this can happen to any of us, to varying degrees. If you feel guilty about something, the easiest way to deflect it is to blame the other person or show anger at being doubted. The red face and bluster of an angry person can sometimes hide the red face and bluster of someone who is actually extremely embarrassed and is trying to think on their feet of a way to divert attention while they gather themselves together. How many times have you seen road accidents, where the person clearly in the wrong launches out of their vehicle and immediately points the finger at the innocent party?

There will be times when you feel embarrassed or ashamed and want to hide away and work it out in private. In situations where that is not possible, you try to save face by being angry. Because the typical response to that is for others to try to placate or calm the situation down, the original reason for the anger can get caught up and lost in the need to restore calm.

To be clear, I am mostly talking here about when you need to ease the discomfort of feeling guilty – in particular when you are glued by guilt that originated from others. When it is positive guilt, you may experience softer emotions such as sadness, regret, or remorse as you start to process what has happened and are able to start creating alternative viewpoints and perspectives.

Your emotional stability is based on being able to interpret and predict the responses and reactions of yourself and others and guilt will make you doubt both. You struggle to feel comfortable with the decisions and choices you have made, because you maybe didn't get the reaction from others that you expected. With that out of balance, your mental sharpness and energy are constantly busy trying to work out what the misalignment is, instead of focusing on just living your life in your own way. Left long enough, it can create physical symptoms that are the body's final way of letting you know that something is not right. Your physical wellness is key to this house of cards staying up – you will know this because if you feel ill or run down, then it can be very difficult to keep motivated and active, going about your day.

In order to strengthen all three, you need to get the emotional and mental aspects strengthened and resilient, by using the following strategies. This inevitably allows your body to remain strong and not fall to illness, disease or physical exhaustion. Live the person you are, with your own set of rules guiding you, and your mind, body and emotional core will keep working hard for you.

# 5:  Guilt as a Positive Emotion

L et's recap on why you should pay attention to some types of guilt that you feel.  Guilt can be positive when it is the Guilt That Moves You – where the emotion is intense, but you feel that you have to take action – there is no avoiding or ignoring it.  This is because the guilt originates from a mismatch between the actions or decisions you take, and your personal moral and ethical code.

### What is your Personal Code?

From birth, you are on a steep and precarious learning curve.  First you learn how to survive, by creating a bond with your primary caregivers to feed, clothe and protect you until you are able to be more independent.  You may start by crying uncontrollably until someone comes to see what you need, but it doesn't take long for you to work out other ways of getting what you want or need.  Through this time, you work out how to behave so that you continue to receive the care you need, and you may already start putting together an idea of what is good behaviour and what is bad.

As everything is aimed at staying alive, you learn the actions and choices that are going to keep that care coming.  I remember my daughters eagerly showing me pictures they had drawn, or telling me long accounts of what they had done at school, each one followed by "am I being a good girl?"  Even as toddlers, children learn to play nicely and be good.  If they don't, then there is a risk that the care and attention they need will be taken away, which they can't let happen.

There is also the flipside of this, that parents can rely on the child learning the rules to encourage good behaviour.  If the amount and kind

45

of attention you give to your child is based on their behaviour being appropriate, then you can show them the correct behaviour that is expected.

A common discipline technique is the naughty step (I used the naughty corner as I sometimes was in places with no steps). This is where you place the child on the step / in the corner and give them some time where they are on their own. Often you are advised not to communicate with the child during the 'time out', so it is a disconnection from the care and affection that they usually get. The theory is that they will use this time to think about their actions, and be able to consider the alternative, correct behaviour that was expected.

For many children this level of maturity and complexity is simply not there, and without the appropriate parental responses, the time out is more clearly a guilt trip scenario. It is telling children that they must act a certain way or the love and affection they seek will be taken away. For children, the rules that they must follow to continue getting care and attention begin to get set very early on, and each time they break rule – intentionally or not – the rules get refined so that they become clear on what is allowed and what is not. If the child intentionally or unintentionally breaks the rules, they feel guilty for disappointing their parents.

To be clear, this isn't an obvious rule book that parents create. It's not as if the parents sit down at any point and work out the Rules of Living in This Family. Instead, it's small adjustments to behaviour that get refined and defined a little each time, until the child is able to predict the reaction they will get from their parent before they take the action.

How much affection the child gets outside of moments of discipline is also extremely important. If a child is constantly reassured and comforted, and they know that they are unconditionally loved, then those moments of discipline are more starkly in contrast to what they are used to, and they know very quickly that something is not right. Handled badly, a child in this scenario can develop a lot of anxiety as they fear the loss of the affection (even when it is clear that love is showered over them at all other times).

The mismatch between their normal environment and that when they are disciplined is so different that it can cause them to constantly be on alert for the sign that the love is going to be withdrawn. As I said, I used the naughty corner with my children, but I tried to make it a learning experience rather than punishment. My approach was to talk to them after the timeout and I would ask them why they were put in the corner, what they thought they maybe could have done differently, and why that mattered. I would ask them to apologise for the action they had taken which needed to be corrected and made sure that they connected the action with the naughty corner.

As an adult it is easy to assume that a child knows which part of their behaviour was inappropriate, but they do not. Many times, I would ask my daughters why they had been put in the naughty corner and they just looked at me blankly. Left at that, the whole experience is simply punishment. As I talked to them and explained what action caused the timeout, they were able to understand and ask questions as to why that was not good behaviour. You can teach children to say sorry, but the power comes in teaching them to say sorry for what, because it helps them refine their rule books.

This might sound a lot for a young child (and my expectations of the answers were always very low) but they got used to knowing that the questions would be asked and so they actually would use the time out to think about what they had done. And immediately after, I would cuddle them, tell them I loved them, and we would carry on as if the discipline hadn't happened. This is an important step and one I would like to explain a little more, particularly in relation to feeling guilty.

As a parent, you are initially taking the role of their personal code or rule book, trying to instil in them some beliefs and values that you feel are important. In this, at the point where their actions are not in line with that code, you have the ability to discipline or show them an alternative action. The approach I took was to make the discipline short but meaningful, so they knew very quickly that something wasn't right, but directly after we had cleared it up, life carried on as before.

This is, in essence how 'good guilt' works – you get immediate feedback that your actions are not in line with what you expect, which gives you an opportunity to understand what is out of kilter and to correct it immediately. Just as important is the ability to learn the lesson as required and move on without further distress or self-punishment. Things will happen, and you will get some things wrong, but the real damage is done by continuing to punish yourself even after everything has been put right.

That damage can be seen if we continue to use the example of the naughty step scenarios. The other options, I believe, do not give that same opportunity to correct course and heal. For example, maybe your child took action and you went through these steps, but you just couldn't let it go, and remained cross with them after (sometimes long after) the incident is over. What is the rule that you are telling your child at that point? Is it, "However much you are sorry for what you did, I get to control when you can start feeling better about it, and I want you to feel bad for a while longer"? The child then learns that once they have done something wrong, they 'deserve' to feel bad for a long time after the apologies are given, and the punishment carried out. As an adult, this will lead them to feel bad long after the incident, even if the person no longer is upset with them.

The other option is that you discipline your child, but you feel so awful for doing so that you overcompensate and try to make amends for disciplining them. I have seen parents who have used the naughty corner and once the timeout is finished, take their child for a cake or a toy to make up for putting them there. And I understand why – it is very difficult to discipline a child who you know just didn't know any better, and you do of course have to make sure that the punishment is appropriate for the action. But again, what does this teach the child? That there was punishment and reward at the same time? That holding someone accountable for their actions makes you the guilty one? Does it show them how to make others feel guilty (my daughter used to have real puppy dog eyes when she sat there, it broke my heart). Imagine yourself as the child in this situation. Can you recognise times in your own life when you have written the rule book following these two options? How has it affected your ability to deal with mistakes you have made?

As a child and as an adult, you will realise that when things go wrong, or you make a mistake, the correction of the behaviour has to be proportionate to the action itself and dealt with as quickly as possible. This teaches you that you need to think about your actions and how they affect others, but also that there are ways of correcting that behaviour and to learn from the experience. It teaches you that guilt can inspire better behaviour.

As you grow and mature, parental guidance on behaviour is joined by guidance from teachers and other adults as well, but you will also have started to use your own judgement and beliefs to direct your actions, and the direction from other adults may not be needed or appreciated.

The argument of nature and nurture is a difficult one – as a child, you have nothing else to go on but the guidance (or lack of guidance) from your parents, and therefore, your belief in their rules of behaviour were nurtured as you grew up. However, even with that guidance, you have a central guidance system, a personal code or a set of values and these become more dominant as you learn how to interpret it all together.

For example, a love of animals may be something that is encouraged by parents, but a child's temperament will determine how that love of animals get represented. Some children immediately go towards animals, others immediately back away. Parents are able to guide some of that response, but not all - as a mother of a daughter who has been scared of animals for most of her life, I can definitely say a parent's reassurances cannot override an internal belief that easily.

Consider as well how each of us responds differently to the same set of circumstances. Think of the story of two brothers – one says, "My father was an alcoholic, therefore I am an alcoholic"; the other says "My father was an alcoholic, therefore I am teetotal". The same situation was interpreted in two completely different ways, based on the values and beliefs of the individual.

That internal code of values and beliefs gets built up over your lifetime and is adjusted as you navigate a variety of situations and deal with different people., each of whom will have their own personal code. This code will be based on your experience of taking action, having a response to that action from yourself and others, and understanding whether it represents the person you want to be. If it doesn't, you will adjust your behaviour, learn from the experience and know better for next time.

You may initially look for acceptance from your parents so that you could survive, but as you grow up, it becomes more important to get acceptance from the wider social group, and so you start seeking reassurance and the new rules of the road from friends, colleagues and society at large.

From school onwards, you watch others closely, looking for clues as to how to behave and be accepted and this stage is critical for you to leave the family dynamic and become your own person in the community. The challenge is to maintain a level of critical analysis over the rules that others give you, and check whether or not to incorporate them into your personal code. This involves watching others as they take action or make decisions, checking their decision alongside your personal code to see what you would have done, trying to understand their reasoning and logic process and possibly reviewing whether or not you would have come to the same conclusion.

For example, you hear from a friend that they cheated on a test in school. You imagine the scenario, and immediately check this action against your own personal code. If integrity is important to you, then you may conclude that you would never cheat on a test in this way. Because it would feel so uncomfortable and illogical to you, you may ask them to explain why they did it. Depending on how they answer, you judge whether your original response still holds, or whether, in those circumstances, you may change your mind.

This is an important process, because it helps you understand yourself and others better. It may mean that you distance yourself from that friend - if their reasoning is completely at odds with your own beliefs and values, you may feel that you no longer have enough in common with them. But it may also mean that you commit to spending a lot *more* time together and get even closer - if you could see that your friend was devastated and felt guilty about cheating, that it was also against their own personal code and they need help to correct the behaviour, they are then demonstrating that they are in alignment with your own code. In this instance, they may feel compelled to admit the cheating, or at least study harder for the next test.

But how do you know that you are feeling guilty for the right reasons? How do you know that you will never cheat on a test and whether that would be because of your personal code or because your parents will be furious? It is critical that you can tell the difference between this internal guilt based on your personal code and the external guilt based on others trying to tell you what your personal code should be.

Living to your personal code is empowering - it demonstrates a growing maturity and an increasing emotional intelligence about the world. Living your life according to other people's rulebooks weakens you by destroying your ability to make your own decisions and choices, for fear of offending someone or displeasing them.  If you are more concerned with upsetting someone than speaking your truth, you've gone too far into *their* rules for *your* life.

I want to now walk you through my process for identifying what type of guilt you are feeling – is it Guilt That Moves You or Guilt That Glues You?

Depending on how you answer this question, influences your next best step:

### What Do I Feel Guilty About?

If you do something and guilt is immediately triggered, this question is fairly easy to answer.  Remember that you don't want to hold onto the guilty feeling for too long if you can help it, so you should ask this question as soon as you start feeling guilty.  But how do you know it is guilt?

Pay close attention to your emotional and physical signs as these will show you how the guilt shows itself to you:

-   Do you flush red?
-   Does your heart race?
-   Do you start sweating?
-   Does your throat constrict?
-   Do you start to feel like crying?
-   Does your stomach turn?
-   Does your breathing go shallow?

You will notice that many of these symptoms are similar to those fight or flight responses that you have when you are scared, angry or stressed.

By understanding the signals of when you are feeling guilty, you can trigger this process off really early and hopefully avoid staying in that heightened state for too long.  It is important to remember that you are not supposed to feel any emotion for long periods of time – they are a *temporary* response to a situation that you deal with and then move on.

But sometimes, guilt isn't immediately obvious. It sometimes hides in the shadows, influencing your decisions but never really showing itself. Because of this, it may also be that you can miss or overlook the signs listed above, because they are mixed in with other things that are going on at the same time. If you are feeling scared or fearful while feeling guilty, how would you tell them apart?

As guilt acts as the filter over every other emotion, it can be difficult to see it straight away, but the next question to ask is:

## What am I telling myself?

Listening to your own internal self-talk can provide meaningful insight into the way you are judging yourself, so start paying close attention to your mind chatter. Watching how you talk to yourself – whether you are positive and supportive, or negative and destructive – can tell you a lot about the emotion that is driving those thoughts.

It can be helpful for you, when journaling, to make a list of statements that you say to yourself, particularly those that get repeated on a regular basis. For example, you might notice that you keep telling yourself that you are always late, that you are eating too much, or that you forget birthdays. Do you find that as you remember different events, you comment to yourself about your likelihood of being successful at that endeavour?

Although these don't immediately spring out as signs of feeling guilty, if you look closely, behind each of these types of statements is a subtext of unworthiness, which in itself is a classic sign of guilt, of not being good enough. If you tell yourself you are always late to appointments, the subtext of that says that you are 'wrong' for being disrespectful to those who are waiting for you (and who, you may imagine, would be disappointed in you for it). If you say that you are eating too much, the subtext is that you are unable to do the 'right' thing of eating appropriately portion sizes.

Look out for these subtexts because at the heart of all of them is the sense that your actions are incorrect for the situation and most importantly, that you should have known better. It is the subtext that answers the questions, "What Do I Feel Guilty About?"

It is really important when you ask this question to be as brutally honest as you can.  Don't skirt around the edges of how you are feeling or try to edit the description of why you feel guilty.  It is tempting to try to neutralise the emotion by playing it down, by making it seem insignificant.  But for the process to work and for you to stop feeling guilty, you have to be completely honest with yourself about just how much guilt there is.  Yes, this time you are late, but if it is on the back of being late the last ten times you met this particular friend, that is a lot of guilt that has built up each time you didn't make it on time.  So, talk about it all.  Own *all* of the guilt that you feel and allow yourself to describe it in all its glory.  Though this is uncomfortable, it is necessary – guilt thrives when you do not face it, because once visible, it is impossible to ignore it.

Next, you need to ask the follow up question:

### What Do I Want to Do About It?

Once the guilt has nowhere to hide and is out in the open, you now have a choice to make about what to do with it.  This choice will ultimately depend on answering this question – *what do I want to do about it?*

Remember, there are two types of guilt – healthy, positive guilt and unhealthy, damaging guilt.  The way to tell the difference between the two is to look at the way that you want to respond to feeling the guilt.

When you ask yourself this question, try to go with the very first response you have to it – it is easy to feel like there is a 'right' answer to it, but there really isn't – just your answer.   If you find that you draw a complete blank when asked what you want to do, then it is likely to be guilt that glues, i.e. the external, negative guilt that is being imposed upon you by others and their expectations.  The reason for the blank is obvious – if it originates from someone else, then they also have to tell you what your appropriate response should be.  Think about when you learn to drive a car.  At the beginning, you don't know any of the controls, so you can't know the next step because they haven't told you yet.
A lot of guilt starts from here – from being told that what you are doing is 'wrong' but not being given the 'right' thing to do.  In the absence of the right answer, you won't know what to do next.  This is **guilt that**

**glues you**, as it glues you in place until someone else tells you the next step.

You may find that your answer to the question is a battle between logic and emotion. Logically, you may know what the appropriate action to take it – but you don't want to. Now you are glued in place but not because you don't know what to do but because you don't want to do it!

Finding out why that is can be very telling – picture a child who snatched a toy from another. They are told to give it back, but they want to keep it. Eventually they are persuaded to return the toy, but they do so stony faced or crying their eyes out because it is definitely against their wishes. This is *also* guilt that glues – even though you know the action you should take, you are not motivated to do so, and so you don't act as you should, instead battling it out inside as to which side of you wins.

Think about the times when you maybe squabbled with your friends, both thinking that you were right. You want to say sorry and repair the friendship, but it is very difficult to get past the need to hear that you were right, and they were wrong. Instead, there is an ongoing 'they said, you said' communication with mutual friends as you try to state your case and 'win' in their eyes. The whole situation could be resolved by talking directly to your friend and apologising, but you don't feel that you should, so you don't.

You can see how damaging this type of scenario can be and why it is gluing you to taking no action. The guilt you feel is therefore not entirely 'your' guilt – there may be elements of the argument that you do feel bad for (maybe you were inconsiderate or hurtful) but there are also elements that you do not feel guilty for (the reason for the argument may be because you were hurt first) and so you can't move forward clearly.

It's important to recognise this – sometimes you will feel guilty for more than one reason at a time, and as such, will have a different answer to this question for each component of the situation. This is why the first question "*What do I feel guilty for?*" needs to be answered as completely as possible. By picking through how you feel, and identifying each aspect of the guilt you feel, you can then answer this second question more easily, and may be able to be understood better why taking the next step feels so difficult for you.

The final answer you may give to the question may be that you feel compelled to act, to make amends and to adjust your behaviour.  This is **guilt that moves you**, because the feeling of guilt is so strong that you cannot rest until you have corrected course and sorted things out.

This is positive guilt, because it is in response to feeling that you have gone against your own personal code, and that you have not represented yourself as you would like to do.  Here is where you will know exactly the right action to take – but that still may not be easy, and you may still find some resistance.  After all, it is incredibly difficult to admit if you are in the wrong, or that you have hurt someone.

You may even find that there are some times where your guilt is for something that has actually affected no-one, but still goes against your code.  I'm not ashamed to admit that I am that person who goes through a clothes shop and has to pick up clothes that have dropped from hangers even when I had absolutely nothing to do with it – it's as if once I've seen it on the floor, I'm complicit.  Obviously, someone would have been affected in this instance – the shop assistant would have had to pick it up instead – but that wasn't something that I caused.

And this is how positive guilt, guilt that moves you, operates.  Because it is tied into your personal code, you have no choice but to correct behaviour, and will find it very difficult to ignore or suppress for very long.

I do want to just make something very clear – feeling compelled to act when you feel guilty *does not* automatically lead to an apology.  Just because your alarm bells are ringing about your behaviour, it does not automatically mean that you were in the wrong or that you should apologise.   But you do need to work out what your honest reaction should be.

For example, as long-term relationships break down, it is common that the couple bicker and fight over sometimes very silly things.  In this case, what one partner says may, in itself, be hurtful and not the way they want to behave, but the true reaction may be to finally come to the realization that the relationship is over.   It's common when relationships reach this stage for the couple to start to peer into the unknown future and then back away. They suddenly fast forward to a future where they are apart and the risk of not finding someone else and being left instead on their own. The fear of that may well be more powerful than the guilt being experienced and so they won't act on it - but this only delays the inevitable.

Guilt is complicated, and you are never feeling guilty over just one thing, so you have to tease apart each of the individual strands and understand what the whole situation is really telling you. If you are arguing with your partner, and the relationship is no longer healthy, then saying sorry for arguing over silly things may be appropriate, but it may need to be tied in with the affirmation that you are better off apart.

This is a key element of living guilt free. Being able to prise apart the different strands of guilt that you may be feeling, to pick through and know what is originating from your personal code and what is being imposed on you is essential in making sure you only act on those things that you want to and do not respond as others expect you to. Your actions will always have some type of impact or consequence and it is really important that you can recognize those that stop you from showing the person you are, and those that stop you from showing the person others want you to be.

It is hopefully becoming clear that when considering the next action that you could take, it may not be just a direct response to the moment. It may have triggered you into thinking about the whole situation and will try to come up with a solution that feels right to your personal code. It is still inspiring you into action and you will still feel that you have to do something in response, to deal with the guilt in a positive way. But you don't want to spend your time responding and reacting to your actions, so what could you do that could help you predict and pre-empt situations where your personal code is going to be tested?

Rather than have to always use this approach for when the guilt has shown itself, you can deepen your self-awareness. You can already see what type of situations or circumstances are going to potentially put you in a situation where you could make a choice that is not in line with your personal code. This means you can prepare particular responses, rather than just waiting for them to happen.

Say for example you have noticed that you make some pretty poor choices of actions and words when you have had a drink, or when you are with a particular group of friends. There have been occasions where you have had to deal with a excruciating hangover the next morning, as well as the shame and embarrassment and guilt of things that you said or did the night before. If it has already happened, then you can use this process to help you work out what your next best move should be – maybe you need to apologise to someone, or even pay some money towards something that was damaged or messed up. But wouldn't it be better if the situation hadn't occurred in the first place? This is where you can learn from previous mistakes and start to change your behaviour before it happens again. This helps with you feeling more in control of your life and also how others perceive you. If you repeatedly end up in this situation, before long the guilt will be triggered way before the night out – as you see the text come in organising the following weekend, or the follow up texts where your friends are already wondering what 'crazy' thing you'll do now.

If you are feeling guilty before you've even done anything, then this is a good time to do some pre-emptive awareness and make a different choice, one that is far more in line with your personal code. Ask a friend to stop you drinking certain drinks or ask them to stop you after a certain number. Make it clear to your friends that you don't want to be 'that' friend anymore and ask for their help in stopping you from going too far. Draw a line in the sand and reset your behaviour to the person you want to see in the mirror the next morning.

But this self-reflection has to be as honest as possible and that includes asking why you think you might drink to excess even when you know that you will feel bad the next day. What is the drinking offering you? Is it about the drink – or about the people? I have had clients who have found that they only take certain actions with a particular group of friends, and the true difficulty and challenge in living without the guilt is to accept that the group of friends is not good for them. They instinctively know that if they really do not want to drink and become out of control, that they need to avoid being with that group and that can be a tough call to make. Think about if you ask these friends to help you not drink as much and they don't want to, or feel that you would be 'less fun' if you didn't get as drunk – are these really the friends who want to know the best you?

As much as social connections, friendships and relationships are essential to your emotional and mental health, this is only the case when they are not destructive or harmful to you. Your links to others should allow you to show the true you and to live by your own personal code without judgement or rebuke.

The voice of your personal code that speaks through the emotion of guilt is a powerful ally in living your life honestly and authentically. You should build a connection with it so that you know that when you feel it, it is because you are not sticking to your code. This does not mean that you isolate or disassociate from others – in fact, quite the opposite.

Wanting to live to your own code helps you grow and develop your empathy and compassion towards others – by wanting to be understood yourself, you are more open to understanding others in all of their complexity. It can help you become an inspirational role model to those around you, who see that you are joyful in living to your code and that it has empowered you in a way that lifts you up but doesn't automatically drag others down.

You are not climbing on the shoulders of others, but instead you are providing a guiding light, showing them the way towards greater self-acceptance and a higher degree of integrity. If you hold yourself accountable for what you say and do, then others learn that you are the true image of yourself and they can rely on you in a way that is both admirable and testament that they too can live as themselves without judgment.

# 6:  Destructive Guilt

D id you have an answer to the question *"What do I want to do now"*?  If you were unsure of what to do or you felt untethered then the chances are that the guilt you are feeling is external, meaning that it originated from someone or something else.  This is an important concept to get your head around, because it illustrates why there is guilt that hangs around you, that stays regardless of what you do and feels impossible to shift.

Let's take a look at body issues, or guilt over how you look.  The chances of you having created that particular narrative are incredibly small, because your internal personal code is concerned with *who* you are, not what you look like.  It may be that you want to be accepted by others – meaning that you appear to be someone that they want to get to know – but the skewered perspective on this is when you think that you *have* to look a certain way to be accepted or found to be worth paying attention to.

Most of your thoughts on how you look are based on a comparison that you do against other people who you feel have been accepted in a way that you would like for yourself.  You therefore try to emulate that look by wearing certain clothes, using certain makeup or dieting in order to hit particular weights or body measurements.  When you can't look like them regardless of what you do, there's guilt that you have somehow got it wrong and that your value to other people is diminished.

Apart from the fact I could write another entire book just on the guilt associated with body image and attractiveness, I want to focus on how this example illustrates the way external guilt plays on your mind and forces you into the 'analysis paralysis' of doubt and uncertainty.

Say you're lonely and have been looking for a new partner but have not been having any luck.  You've decided that it might be because of the way you look and present yourself.  So you have read articles and seen the social media clips of people who seem to have overcome the same issue, and you look to see if there is anything that you can learn from them on how to maybe increase your chances. You binge-read every article that tells you the key aspects of finding true love – the self-help work that you need to do, the products and opportunities that have worked for other people - and so you decide that if it has worked for them, you will give it a go.

You buy the makeup, you go for a new hairstyle, and you buy the outfits that – they say – will guarantee you a partner. You read the books, attend the workshops and say the affirmations that - they say - will make you more confident. You go onto the dating site, update your photos to show this new, attractive and sexy you, with a snappy bio that - they say - encapsulates your most endearing qualities. But the people you are wanting to connect with are still not selecting you. By now, you have tried all of these different ways of changing your luck, and you begin to feel guilty that you have somehow got it wrong. It must be you doing something wrong, because these other people all found love, right?

Wrong. There are so many other reasons why people find their partners, and whilst the way they look might catch the attention, it is much deeper than that. You find love and companionship by finding someone with common interests and viewpoints, who laughs at your jokes, or who sits up with you until early morning discussing your favourite movies. But the information you have read has all been based on the incorrect notion that it is about how you present yourself and not who you are on the inside. There are no special tricks that you can learn from others, but it doesn't stop you thinking that there are.

And this is not your fault either. There are entire industries based on you believing that there are people 'out there' that know more about what will make you happy than you do, and you are sold the possibility that they can give it to you. You cannot know which of the above things you did were having the desired effect for those individuals because the reason for their success in love may have had nothing to do with any of the things that they have told you about. They didn't find love because they chose the right colour lipstick or wore the right length skirt.

The reason for success in love is absolutely unique to everyone and because of that the only valuable work you can do is on knowing who you are and what makes you happy. But doing the real work of finding yourself is not for the faint hearted. In comparison to wearing a longer lasting lipstick, figuring out who you are and being okay with that is seriously long and arduous work. More importantly, it will show you that there are no short cuts, that there is no price tag you can associate with doing the work. A quicker and simpler response than doing the inevitable self-reflection is to believe that you did something wrong and that you need someone or something else to help you fix it.

The guilt from this situation is because you continue to believe that they have a solution to the problem, and that you are doing something wrong which is why it is not working. And I completely understand that logic – you are being told that these methods work, yet you're not seeing the results that others have – so it has to be you, right?

Let's change the example a bit to show you just how easy it is to fall for this logic. Imagine that you have finally decided to clean the water stains on your bath with the new wonder product that 'guarantees' to clear it with one application over 15 minutes. And the advert contains lots of delighted people all telling you how easy it was for them to get rid of their stains, and there are countless images of before and after shots of baths with various levels of grime being magicked away. You're quite sceptical that it will work as well as they say, but you are desperate and so you order some.

When you get it, you immediately go upstairs and spray it into your bath tub. You set the alarm for 15 minutes and fully anticipate hearing angels singing as this product clears away decades of a dripping tap. The alarm goes off, you get your cloth and begin to wipe away the product, and hopefully, the stain. But you see that the stain doesn't look as if it has been touched. In fact, apart from now being the colour of the liquid that you sprayed on it, it looks exactly as it did before.

In this example, what would you say your response is – do you realise that the advert wasn't an accurate reflection of how effective it would be? Or do you decide to rub it a little bit harder, re-read the instructions in case you missed a section, change the cloth you are using to a scouring pad, or spray it on and leave it on for longer, maybe even overnight? Would you consider the question "*maybe I'm doing something wrong?*"

The logic you use to convince yourself that doing x, y and z will give you the results you are after does not come from you, and so when it doesn't work there is only so much problem solving you are able to do before you run out of ideas. It looked successful for other people, and it looked like they had solved it in such a way that they could pass on their wisdom and you could benefit from that. You have skipped to the solution provided by someone else and now you are unable to understand which part isn't working.

In this case, the only option you have is to haphazardly try changing things around and see if it makes a difference – or you wait for the people who have got it all figured out to come back and tell you what you are doing wrong. This usually ends up being a new product or item that they now say, with complete confidence, is the best way to get the results you are after. Hence the reason every house has a cupboard full of cleaning products and a drawer full of miracle face creams.

Whether you are talking about dating tips or cleaning products, the mechanism is the same – someone tells you that they have the correct answer on a particular subject and that you can get the same results. This is all advertising is, really – somebody saying that they have the solution to your problem. But it is easy for you to then attach guilt to when it doesn't work like that for you. Instead of seeing that the product is not as advertised, you may see the evidence that shows it is working for some people, and start to point the finger of blame at yourself.

When the solution does not work for you, the assumption is that you have done something wrong, not that it was never going to work for you because it didn't and couldn't take into account your own circumstances and context. This assumption can be insinuated by others when you question them but also by your own logic. When you hear someone tell you the 'right' answer, particularly if it is said with complete authority, or said by someone who you trust, you immediately give what they are saying more weight and authority over your own mind.

This situation is difficult enough, but there is another complexity that leads to the inability to make the next right step. Let's remind ourselves of the two undisputed truths in the world of social dynamics:

*1 – Everyone will have an opinion*
*2 – Every opinion will be different.*

These truths lead you to the possibility that you feel guilty but cannot understand the 'right' way to change course, to correct behaviour. Remember that when guilt **moves** you, there is a compulsion to act, to make adjustments so that you are back in line with your personal code. And critically, you know what those adjustments should be because they are based on an internal wisdom of what the right thing to do is.

When you are experiencing external guilt – the guilt that **glues** you – the guilt still wants to make you act but you have no idea what the next right action is because you didn't come up with the original action. Now, you have everyone telling you different and mainly conflicting ideas that - they say - are the right ones. But not everybody can be right! The people giving you their opinion are usually stating it as fact, as if only they have the right response.

So, what do you do? You get caught up in trying to figure out which option makes the most sense, but because your initial actions were based on the opinions of others, you have no idea whether to continue following the original set of ideas, or whether you need to try something new. All in all, trying to get your head around what to do next, whilst still feeling the debilitating pressure of guilt makes you extremely uncomfortable and makes you doubt your ability to make the right call.

This is why external guilt has such an impact on your self-confidence and self-worth. They are critically damaged by this logic that you don't know the right answer and so have to wait to be told by others. Think about a scenario where you feel really confident. Maybe it is at work, or with a group of friends. Your confidence comes because you *know* what you are doing – your skill set is honed and refined, or you simply trust those people so much that you feel comfortable showing the true you to them.

But then think of a situation where you are questioning yourself. Maybe you are out of comfort zone and surrounded by those who are telling you that they know better. With nothing to anchor yourself to – with no absolute knowledge, or belief that you can learn – you are likely to capitulate to them, to give in to their decisions and opinions and, critically, start to doubt your ability to make the same good choices.

Say you've started a new job. You know that you are able to do the job, but there are some processes and systems that you need to learn, as you haven't used them yet. Depending on your level of confidence at that time, and the personalities of your new colleagues, you can find yourself in a situation where all of your expertise is questioned because you don't know how to immediately work the system.

It is not unusual to start a job and feel a little out of your depth – that's natural and a part of making sure you are being challenged and stretched. But stay there too long and it is extremely difficult to then convince people that you're the expert that you are. You start hearing the 'you should know this by now", or "do you still not know how to do this?" and you begin to think that they know more than you about everything, not just those procedural issues. And if your colleagues are not saying it to you, it's almost guaranteed that you've started saying it to yourself.

This is how external guilt works. It puts into your head that others know better than you about what you need to do, and that throws your logic off into a complete rollercoaster. Now your brain doesn't go to your own abilities, skills and experience to get the right next move. It goes to the part of your brain that holds everyone else's opinion of what you should do and instead of asking for the 'right' answer, it asks for the answer from the person who you want to impress or get approval from the most. Every wondered why some people's faces pop into your head as you think of what you should do? That's what's going on – you are replaying their choices and decisions to know what you should do, to keep them happy.

Depending on how long you have wanted that person's approval or acceptance, it may not feel like guilt any more, and it may not ever be spoken by them. Maybe you have wanted your parent's approval for your choice of partner. Maybe you want your partner's support on your career ambitions. Maybe you've always wanted to be accepted by the cool kids at school. Whatever the driver, the need to get their acceptance or approval overrides your own ability to make the decision for yourself.

In many cases, these people don't even know that they are making you feel guilty. You may have gained an idea of what their 'right' answers are by watching them, by listening to how they talk about themselves and judgments that they may have made about others. Putting all of this together you have created a view of what you think they are looking for, and so begin to act accordingly. When you don't get it right, or you feel that you missed the target, you start to feel guilty for letting them down, even though they may never say that or insinuate it in any way.

How many times do you make yourself appear the way that you think others want to see you, only to find out that it isn't? Potential partners don't find you attractive for playing a part – they are attracted to seeing the real person, and the further away you are from that, the less they will be interested. Potential friends won't want to get to know you because you've binge-watched all of the latest boxsets if you clearly didn't enjoy any of them or remember any of the details. Potential hiring managers won't hire you because of how you look or behave in an interview if your key skills and qualities are not what they are looking for.

Trying to give others what they are looking for doesn't work but sets you up to feel continually guilty about not attaining a particular standard, that doesn't even really exist to those that you are trying to please.

While this is true in a majority of cases, it is important to also be able to identify where there are people *deliberately* trying to control you by using these little guilt trips in order to adapt and change your behaviour. While there are many people who you allow to influence you who do not mean to, there are also a few people who realise that making you feel guilty is a quick but effective way to get you to change your actions to suit their purposes, not yours. And I'd love to say that these are people who you can easily remove from your life for their damaging impact on your confidence and value but unfortunately it is also true that these tend to be those in close relationships with you, be it partners or family members.

When you love someone, or you have a familial bond to them, there are huge expectations and assumptions made about how much you try to share your life with them. For family, you can assume that this is a bond that ties you to them forever. On top of your own personal code you may have a family code of behaviour that is expected – and they do not always match up.

Think of the rebellious teenagers or children who go against parents' wishes – as you grow up, your views on the world and your perspective is shaped by more than your parents and family, and it is not unusual for you to start moving away from them. One of the quickest options families have to get you back in line is to make you feel guilty about moving away from them (either physically or mentally) and begin to question the family bond if you continue to do that.

Sometimes this process has started very early on, with parents maybe pretend crying to their children when the child does something 'wrong' – this sets the rule for the child that they are capable of hurting their parents which to a child is unthinkable. And the threat of having their unconditional love being taken away can make children act however you want them to in order to stay in your good books, but many later rebel against this level of control over them.

Because of how long these techniques may have been used, you may be unaware that you are even being drawn into a guilt trip. The logic you use could be broken down into something like this: "*if I do x, it will disappoint my mother and she may pull her love away from me as she used to when I was naughty as a child, and so I definitely don't want to upset my mother and it feels like it is against my personal code*". This can become so automatic that you no longer break it down and instead you go straight to "it's against my personal code" and think that it is internal guilt.

This can also be more confused by the fact that you may hold family ties very strongly in your personal code and may actually feel that you do not want to upset your mother because you love your family – but that doesn't mean that part of the guilt trip is not based on your mother learning that this is important to you and so using it to make you change your behaviour. You have to begin breaking down what you *actually* feel guilty about to tease out those aspects that are others basically piggy-backing your own personal code.

There is not always the logic of "*if I do x, I will disappoint them*". Sometimes it is hidden inside the appearance of support. Take for example, a relationship or marriage, where the woman would like to work after having children, but the partner isn't so keen. In this scenario, the partner could use small guilt trips, such as reminding the woman that she wanted children and so she should be happy to look after them. Or they might argue that the childcare would be prohibitively expensive, and it would not be financially beneficial. Both of these trigger different expectations – one that as a mother your children are your only concern, and one that you should only look to work for financial gain and not for personal satisfaction. Both of these considerations *are* legitimate – but do not make up the whole reason why some women want to return to work. You can be made to feel that you are being selfish for wanting something for yourself, and that you should be happy with your role as mother.

But you are never just one role. Every day you play a plethora of roles at the same time. You don't stop being a daughter or son when you become a wife or husband. And you don't stop being a career person because you become a parent. But it can feel that the choice over which role is most important to you is given to you from others, and particularly in the case of your partner, the influence they have over you can make it feel that you have no way to push back and create the roles that work for you.

Sometimes, you are able to argue your case sufficiently that your partner realises that you are serious about making that choice, whether it be to go back to work, start a new business, or pursue a brand-new item on your bucket list. But this is where they may use a new tactic that, I would suggest, is the most dangerous of all. I call it the Cinderella Syndrome.

Think of the Cinderella story, in particular the wicked step mother. When Cinderella wants to go to the ball, it is expected that the stepmother will continue to reject her wishes and not allow her to attend. Yet the stepmother surprises them all when she agrees that she can go – IF she gets all of her chores done by the time the carriage leaves.

This is a very sly tactic – she is essentially *allowing* Cinderella her choice, but still managing to control the outcome by providing a set of conditions that are pretty much unachievable (particularly when she was aware how much her own daughters would sabotage Cinderella's efforts to meet them). Eventually, although Cinderella did get the work done, it was not done in time and the carriage left without her, her stepmother advising, regretfully, that she hadn't met the conditions of going, as she closes the door.

It may be uncomfortable to suggest that a partner could be as wicked as the stepmother, but the tactic is one that is used by many couples trying to balance the family and work commitments. When the mother wants to return to work, in many cases her partner will agree – as long as the children are still cared for, that she available for any and all child-related emergencies and appointments, and that she continues to maintain the house, keep the cupboards stocked and the food on the table. Here, the mother is being asked to meet conditions that, with the best will in the world, will be nearly impossible to meet at all times. And at the point that she cannot meet them, her partner informs her regretfully that it is *her* fault because she was the one who wanted the career/business/hobby.

When a relationship becomes this unbalanced – when one person can dictate so much of how the relationship is going to work – then there is the potential to have this scenario of being set up to fail. The partner has to do nothing but watch the mother struggle to cope, under the premise that they were not the one who wanted to make life so hard but fails to acknowledge or appreciate the mother's reasons for wanting it.

This is a sign that the relationship has gone from one based on **compromise** to one based on **compliance**, where one partner has more say over how the relationship will continue to exist. This is not a healthy relationship and one that I sadly see represented over social media all of the time, with women reaching out to other women for support on how to cope with a partner who is not doing their fair share of the parenting responsibilities.

Although this is most harmful in relationships, the same kind of pressure can exist in any of the relationships and connections you have. Anyone who is creating a set of conditions against how you want the relationship to work is attempting to control your behaviour and your actions by creating a scenario where you are indeed offered exactly what you want but in such an unachievable way that you are destined to not make it. This then gives them the ability to make you feel guilty about not getting there, and you are more likely to do it their way from that point on.

Guilt over how other people will feel is not useful to you at all. I know that sounds harsh, but it is the truth. Taking action that is defined by the response of others means you are constantly navigating your life through a series of immoveable obstacles, and it is guaranteed that many of them will conflict with each other entirely. Where does that leave you?

The only real way to prepare for dealing with any kind of pressure or conditions, is to set *your own idea* for each role you play in life. If you know what kind of friend, mother, father, daughter, son, husband or wife you want to be, then it is clearer to you when someone else is trying to enforce their choices and decisions onto you. If you recognise it earlier, you are less likely to feel guilty and begin to comply with their wishes before realising that this is not the direction you want to go.

If you don't do this work, if you don't know how you want to play each role, then others will fill the void and tell you – but it will be on their terms. And wicked or not, you allow them to be the stepmother letting you know if you can go to the ball.

The importance of owning and creating the roles that work for you is coming up in Chapter Eight, but for now I want to focus on where you go when you answer the question *"What do I want to do about it"* with a blank. You can see here that this usually means that you are dealing with guilt that is coming from external sources, and so the next important step is to identify what the source is and how you want to handle it going forward.

The main aim is to identify who is inspiring the guilt, but that can be difficult to do when there may be multiple sources or inputs. As I said, everyone has an opinion, and every opinion will be different. So, if this is the case, how can you pick it apart to know just what you are dealing with.

It can help to ask the following questions:

## What Is It I Am Telling Myself?

Sometimes the clue is in the self-talk that gets triggered by the guilt that you are feeling. Is it generic (*"I'm always late"*, *"I can't believe I fell for this again"*) or is it more specific (*"I'm such a bad friend"*, *"what kind of son am I?"*). As you can tell the more specific self-talk would suggest that the origin of the guilt is the person who is the other half of the role that you are playing.  So, are you telling yourself that you are generally in the wrong, or are you imagining individual people or groups of people thinking that you are in the wrong?

## How Do I Feel Guilty?

Again, you are looking for clues as to how the guilt is presenting itself. Do you feel that the situation makes you seem a generally nasty person, or a nasty friend / sister / brother / employee?

It may feel far more generic, as though the world is going to be judging your decision and choices and find you lacking – thanks to social media everyone believes they have the right to provide feedback on your life.

The more you can drill down into what you actually feel guilty for, the more it can provide the clues you need to understand the source of the guilt and therefore whether it is a specific relationship that is triggering it, or a more general sense that you are getting a social norm wrong.

## Who Do I Think of When I Feel Guilty?

Slightly more obvious, you may find that someone's face pops into your head as you feel the guilt start bubbling up.  It may simply be a response to the situation – if you have ghosted a friend recently, and you see a message come in from them, you may picture them immediately and connect the two things together.

But equally, you may find that someone unconnected with the situation gets brought to mind – for example, you may picture your parents as you are running late to your child's parents' evening (because they were never late for yours).

Or you may picture your boss as you see an email ping into your inbox of a piece of work that you forget to get completed (because you know they like everything completed first time on time).

Maybe you don't think of any particular person, but just a sense that the world at large would consider you acting in the wrong way.  You can blame social media for the intensity with which you feel this now, but in reality, society dictating the rights and wrongs of behaviour has been going on since human beings built communities.  On top of the legal and moral codes that are established so that communities don't destroy each other, there are a whole raft of societal norms that influence how you behave. In Victorian times, a lady showing her ankles was considered highly inappropriate, and yet now you would think this type of custom was really odd. Changes are brought about by people knowing the norm but *not* adopting it, offering instead an alternative behaviour or action. This doesn't make them accepted or popular, but if done so with confidence and a willingness to explain why the change is a good idea, you are able to set new trends.

But you have to accept that, for a while, you will be surrounded by disapproval and lots of people trying to get you to conform. Conforming to society's rules can be nearly impossible given that society can't quite seem to make up its mind as to what the norm should be. For every person who says left, others say right. For every mother who breastfeeds, there is another who bottle feeds. For every person for capital punishment, there are those against. For every pro-life supporter, there is a pro-choice supporter. For every cosmetic surgery fan, there is a body positive fan.

Society can't make up its mind what is the right answer, so what hope do you have? And trying to keep 'society' happy will have you going around in ever decreasing circles, until you have no idea what your opinion is on any given subject as you realise that whichever side you come down on, someone will take issue with it and try to use guilt as their mechanism for you switching to their point of view.

## Can I See Why They Think That I Am Wrong?

Once you recognise the person or part of society that is making you feel guilty, then you are able to work out how you want to respond, but that first takes you trying to understand their perspective. This is a really important step, as to decide how to respond you have to first understand and appreciate if there are any elements of what they are saying that you agree with.

As we've discussed a few times so far, guilt is multi-layered, and, in many situations, you will have a combination of some internal guilt, mixed with some external guilt. Some will make you want to take action, some will make you feel stuck in place while you wait for the next sign from others on how to proceed. In order to work out what to listen to and what to ignore, it is helpful to try to put yourself in the position of the other person to see if you can identify with any of the opinion you believe they hold.

Take some time to imagine yourself in a conversation with them, where they tell you exactly why you should feel guilty. Try to be as detailed as you can – keep away from generalisations (*"you always do this"*) and drill down into exactly what they would be upset about (*"you are always late to meet me, and it feels so disrespectful"*).

As you can see, when you break it down, you can begin to see not just the guilt trip or the accusation, but also what might be sitting behind it. Using your knowledge of that person, or what you assume about them in the case of strangers out in society, you can start to separate out which parts may be valid and which you can ignore.

In this example, you may realise that you don't want to be disrespectful because that breaks your personal code; however, you can also see that you are not late every time you meet them, and, in some cases, they have been late for you, so that part of the accusation may not feel valid. The more you can separate them out, you can start to understand what your next best move is, by removing consideration of the parts you don't feel break your code, and this will help trigger the action required to rectify the behaviour that does.

### What Do I Want to Do About This?

This question now become answerable, because you have detached the external unhelpful guilt from the internal meaningful guilt, and you will see you now know what action you need to take. The guilt that is unhelpful gets dealt with by better defining the roles you play, and therefore the rules you are prepared to play by for each one. By being clear on these rules – *your* rules – it is much harder for someone to try to get you following theirs and you become more empowered and in charge of your own life.

Let's delve a bit further into how to tell the difference between Guilt That Moves you and Guilt That Glues You.

# 7:  How to Tell the Difference

G uilt That Moves You – the guilt from inside - can be empowering; Guilt That Glues You - guilt coming from external sources - is disabling.  I wish I could tell you that there is a simple solution – just act on the internal guilt, ignore the external – but you know I would be lying, and you'd stop reading.  Instead I'm going to say this – knowing where it is coming from opens you up to the possibility of dealing with the guilt so that it doesn't keep holding you in a life not of your choosing.  Dealing with it can be taking action, or trying to ignore it but either way, you set yourself on the path to be free of it.

Once you decide to take action, your mind tries to complete the reasoning or story behind that choice.  This is easy to do when it originates from your personal code (although finding the words still may feel difficult), but it is extremely difficult to create something when you weren't the one who put the thought in your head.  When you are swayed by the expectations or opinions of others, you still have to feel that it was your own logic and reasoning that made you act.

In order to be kind to yourself, you therefore unconsciously make everything feel like it is coming from inside – it makes you feel less coerced or compliant.  You are saying to yourself, "I'm not doing it because you want me to, I'm doing it because I want to."  You know that you are just feeding yourself a line, but you can live with that.  You can live with it, that is, until you realise that by taking actions that go along with other people's codes, you are actually getting further and further away from what feels right to you.  The guilt of not following *their* idea of the correct answer is replaced by the guilt of not following your own.

There are several signs that you can pay attention to that can help you identify the origins or source of your guilt.  The main one by far is the answer to that question *"What do I want to do about it?"*  This is the key to understanding whether the guilty feelings are coming from your personal code or from others, and it is all based, as we covered before, by what you feel your next action should be.

Simplified down to absolute essentials – do you feel like doing something about feeling guilty or not? That sounds so easy, and yet it requires such a complicated analysis to answer. You have to be able to be absolutely honest with yourself, which is tough after years of absorbing the views of others, trying to tell yourself that you're in control by taking those views on as your own.

The honesty required to admit what you are really thinking of as you make decisions should not be underestimated – many of the values and beliefs that are not really yours have been bleeding into your psyche for a long time and it will be confusing to try to do this logically and rationally. Your brain has done a brilliant job of convincing you that you take ownership of all of it, so don't be surprised if it won't immediately relinquish this position as you search for your truth.

You won't necessarily get an obvious unmasking of the guilt – you won't suddenly find the layers peel away to expose the opinions of others that have been dressed up as your own. But what will happen is that you will become more adept at working through the confusion to find your true beliefs and choices, and that will make the process begin to speed up each time you are faced with a guilt trip of some kind.

My clients usually tell me that beginning this process is hard and they start by feeling like they simply don't understand what to do or how to ask the questions. They admit that they consciously block trying to answer the question because they *do* already know the answers, but they are just not prepared to go there just yet. Your mind will slowly learn that it is okay to allow you to see the difference between the guilt that moves and the guilt that glues, but initially, you may find that you have to rely on subtler and emotionally driven 'tells' before your brain allows you to see them more clearly.

We discussed earlier what guilt as an emotion can feel like – that deeply uncomfortable, almost physical pain and discomfort that can blind you to everything else you are feeling at the time. I always think it feels like every one of your nerve endings has suddenly been switched on and you are flooded with sensations from everywhere on your body, inside and out. Your brain and body can't decide which of these impulses it needs to pay attention to, and so it tries to do an audit of all of them, a quick check to see if any are life threatening or simply really, really uncomfortable.

The survival instinct kicks in, and your flight or fight response initiates and gets ready to move – but it still requires you to tell it where to go.

Your brain however, cannot make that decision because it is trying to process a million different inputs at the same time, and it feels paralysing as you wait for it to pick one. Emotionally, you will find that you will already have an answer (even if that answer is that you don't know what to do). Emotions happen within the thalamus (part of the limbic system within your brain) before your logical brain can process and assess all of the information, and so your emotional brain will reach a decision long before that point.

Your emotional brain's decision reflects your personal code – it will recognise how much personal ownership and accountability you are prepared to take for the original action. It will want to react in one of two ways:

1. You feel deep personal responsibility, and you will want to correct the situation as soon as possible. It is not reflective of the person you want to be and therefore is internalised guilt;
2. You don't feel a high degree of personal responsibility for the original action and so you are going to rely on what the logical part of your brain deems the right thing to do, once it has caught up. This is external guilt.

Personal ownership and accountability are at the heart of how you experience guilt. You have to draw the link between the action you decided to take and the consequence of that decision. The simpler the connection you can make, the easier it is to see whether it is your responsibility and thus whether the guilt you are feeling is internal and a response to breaking your personal code, or not.

If, at the emotional level, the connection is not as clear, and other factors can be taken into account, then it is harder to take personal accountability as quickly and there is a pause to let the logical brain tell you what to do next. The time between these two parts of your brain working things out are miniscule, but every nanosecond counts, because it is in the pause or hesitation that you get your first clue as to the guilt's origin.
Even when your emotional and logical brains are in sync, and you believe feel guilty because you ignored your personal code, that may

still not be true.  There are times when rules from others have become so embedded in your behaviour that it can feel that they are yours, yet there are still signs when that is not the case.

## Procrastination

Procrastination is an almost certain sign that the guilt you are experiencing is not yours.  When you delay taking action, it is essentially giving yourself space for more thinking time.  Yet, if the guilt originates from your personal internal code, why would you need any more time to think about it?   In truth, you don't.   The delay is because your emotional and logical minds are not yet fully in sync – the rule that you have supposedly broken is not present in your personal code and so therefore, you don't act upon it.

Procrastination can take many forms – maybe you find other things to do, or you convince yourself that the timing of the action is just not right.  Maybe you consider the context or circumstances and feel that it might not have all been down to you – you try to discharge your own discomfort by diverting attention to others who might have been at fault.  When you are trying to delay the behavioural correction – when you are avoiding apologising or taking other remedial action – you are effectively admitting that you don't actually feel as guilty as you feel that you should, or as much as maybe others want you to.

That doesn't necessarily mean that realising this takes away the guilt – or takes away the likelihood that others will try to make you feel accountable and responsible.  But it does mean that you have to be very clear if you do apologise to know exactly what you are apologising for. Even when rules from others are indistinguishable from your own, the lack of heart behind the guilt and the lack of motivation to act quickly to correct course can give you the clue you need to disconnect yourself from the guilt and to examine it further, to see just where it does emanate from.

For example, you forget someone's birthday.  You don't usually forget as the dates are all written in your diary, including this one.  But you see the date get closer and close, and instead of getting ready for it, you just let it go by.  You feel guilty for not getting prepared and then you feel guilty on the day – but you still don't act.  You can maybe see many opportunities during those days to get a card, or send a text, or post on social media.  Yet you didn't take it.  The guilt you are feeling may feel very real, you may blame your lack of organisation skills, a lack of money or time, or you may frame it as another example of you failing at life.  But deep down, the real guilt you are feeling is because you recognise that it didn't actually bother you enough to do something about it.  Depending on whose birthday it was, this could be at odds with familial, friend or relationship expectations from those around you.

Even when something isn't important to you, it can still be very important to other people and that can put you at odds with those closest to you. My grandmother is a stickler for remembering birthdays – we joke that on January 1st she has already written all of the cards for everyone in her address book for the coming year (no joke, she usually has). She has usually given you a card weeks before your birthday, and she reminds you months before everyone else's birthday so that you don't forget.  It is extremely important to her to remember people, but many of them are people that we have personally never met, and so with our busy lives, we forget.

I think we would probably argue as well that given we know that she is going to remind us numerous times beforehand, we don't need to remember them ourselves.  But on many occasions, the cards get forgotten until the last minute and we are scrambling about.  I do always feel guilty for missing a birthday, but I have to be honest here – probably not because of upsetting that specific person.  I realise that they probably have very little idea of who I am and probably only just about know why we are sending them cards, so I don't think they would be distraught if I didn't send them a card.  But I *do* feel guilty for upsetting my grandmother – it may not be important to me, but it is to her and I feel guilty for not respecting that.  Yet every year, without fail – I delay.

## Will Power or 'Want' Power?

The key clash in the decision to take action is between your will power and 'want' power.  What on earth is 'want power'?  Let me explain.

When you don't *want* to do something, but you know you have to, you tend to rely on your will power to force you to take the action required.

Your will power feels strong and you feel in complete control of it, so it is a good mechanism to use to make sure you meet your obligations. But your will power works like a muscle – yes, it can get stronger the more you use it, but it can also get tired, particularly if it is not given a rest of any sort.

This is why making new years' resolutions can be a recipe for disaster – most resolutions are made for things that you know you should do, but that you don't really want to. You are completely reliant on your will power keeping you going. This will work for a while, but it will eventually weaken, and if you haven't thought of a more robust reason for wanting to carry on with it, the will power gives way and you're not only breaking your resolution but probably going all in on making up for lost time. Will power can be used for a short period of time but is literally forcing you to do something that you haven't yet full absorbed as something you really, really want – and eventually, the will gives way.

This is where your 'want' power kicks in – when you want something, truly and deeply, you have made an emotional connection to what achieving that aim will give you. I could set my alarm clock for, say, four o'clock each morning, giving myself plenty of time for exercise, meditation, eating healthily, getting myself primed for a productive day. I choose to do this because I read somewhere that many of the most successful people in the world have this type of regime and I want to be like them, so I will do what they do and see what happens. But I hate mornings. I'm not a morning person – I come alive after ten o'clock at night, rather than rise in the morning with a spring in my step.

So, every day, will power is driving me on, pressing the alarm off button and getting up. And each day, I slowly find it more difficult, until soon, I'm snoozing and drifting back to sleep until the much more respectable but maybe not as productive seven am. My will power is only ever going to get me so far, before my other needs (in this case, sleep) weakens my resolve. And as I finally stop setting the alarm clock for four o'clock, I feel guilty that I haven't been able to keep going and begin that slow drip-feed of negative self-talk that I'm just destined to not be a success.

But maybe, during those first few days, I've noticed that I HAVE become more productive. Maybe I have managed to get some goals achieved that have been ongoing for ages and because the house is so quiet, I've managed to blast through them really quickly.  Maybe I've started to notice that I'm not so tired during the day, or that my fitness levels are starting to improve.  Maybe I have seen I am calmer at handling situations because I've been able to meditate each morning.

With evidence that I *am* getting results in my life that mean something to me, that will power transforms into 'want' power, and now the alarm clock going off isn't a nuisance – in fact, I'm waking up just before it goes off, my mind already buzzing with what I've got planned for the day.  By tying the activity with something that I deeply desired, I no longer need to rely on will power, and I am far less likely to give up because I can now feel the value of it.  And if I don't give up – I don't have the guilt.

If *you* want to do something, then not doing it will make you feel guilty and you won't feel settled until you have started it once again.  If *others* want you to do something, then not doing it will trigger guilt, but this is when procrastination and delay will cut in, and you will have to use your will power to get you going.  And you can now see from the above how successful that is likely to be if you never get to the point where it matches what you want to do.

## Should, Could and Would

If you want to recognise whether your guilt is internal or external, listen to the language you use when describing the action you need to take.  As a coach, I am trained to listen out for those three little words that tell me that you are not totally sold on an idea – **should**, **would** or **could**.

These three terms are an absolute giveaway that you do not want to do something and that there is pressure from others in some way that is forcing you into it.

There is usually a thought process that follows after one of my clients has told me they 'should' do something.  They first give me an answer that seems to be reasonable and logical and fool proof.  Then I ask what would happen if they didn't do it, and they give me, once again, some clear and fool proof consequences.  The main aim of their answers is to get me to back away and stop challenging why they need to do something. The problem is, all of these great responses are delivered in a lacklustre, noncommittal, slightly disconnected way. They say the words but, as my mum would say, the smile doesn't reach the eyes.

You can logically know what the 'right' action is to take, and also describe the impact of not doing it – but you can also still not really want to do it either.

You know this is true. Think about being offered that last glass of wine, just to finish the bottle. "Oh well, I shouldn't, but if you insist …". If at this point you were asked why you shouldn't, you'd have a really good explanation – early rise tomorrow morning, you've already had more than you had planned, you have to be able to get up in the night if your children need you. All good reasons, yet – you still have the glass of wine. This is the **should** principle in a nutshell – it allows you to rationally state the 'right' answer, yet still not feel compelled to do it.

I'm not saying for a minute that this is simple. Even when you know that you're doing something because you feel you 'should', it can still trigger massive feelings of guilt of not complying with the rules that you know you must follow. Many of these rules however are impossible to follow – keeping with the wine theme for the moment, the press has reported that red wine is good and bad for you, and that it will lengthen and shorten your life span. How is it possible that both sides of that are true?

The problem with following the rules because you 'should' is that they contradict each other constantly. They have all been created by different people in different contexts and so you are trying to pacify opposing sides of a debate you don't really understand. Without the essential element – that *you* know why it is important and you WANT to do it – you won't know which way to turn but you will feel guilty throughout.

Most of the Guilt That Glues You is uncovered by picking through your list of 'shoulds'. By identifying those things you feel guilty for, that you feel you should do or say, you can quickly see that you are setting yourself up to fail from the start. You are listening to standards and principles that others say are important, allowing yourself to be influenced and coerced into trying to achieve them and then feeling guilty when you don't get it right. The *real* kicker is when you realise that you feel guilty for failing in something that you never really wanted anyway. What a waste of time!

The word '**could**' is also an indicator that the want and desire is not fully formed. When you use could – for example, "I *could* go for a run" – it is a halfway house between willing yourself and wanting to do something. There is slightly more potential that you will go, as could suggests that you are seeing it as a possibility. However, if that sentence carries on with "I could go for a run, but..." – it's just a should in disguise. What you are effectively saying is that you see why it might be a valid possibility, you are acknowledging its legitimacy, but the desire and commitment is still not really there.

It still allows a small window of opportunity to dodge it, and so it not showing full commitment. However, if you don't go for that run, there is a risk that you will start to say, "I should have gone for a run ..." and begin to feel guilty for making the wrong decision. If you hear yourself say 'I could', ask yourself whether you are able to change the 'could' for 'will', to test immediately how likely it is to happen. Listen to the difference of the two phrases: "I could go for a run", or "I will go for a run". You can see straight away how there is ownership in the second one. If you don't run after saying you will, then you are more likely to struggle with internal guilt because you made a promise to yourself that you broke. The level of accountability that you will have over the second phrase is far higher and therefore no easy escape route out of doing it.

The most blatant sign for not being committed to something is the use of the word '**would**'. Take the phrase "I would go for a run," – you already know there is a 'but' after that don't you? Yes, it acknowledges that you can take that action, but it is pretty obvious that you are not committed to doing so. The explanation or excuse you use after this phrase will indicate how much ownership you are prepared to take and therefore how guilty you would feel if the explanation is accepted.

Walking around the streets of London you get accosted by charity workers with clipboards constantly, trying to get you sign up for some type of monthly donation. It is an intricate dance between the workers who know that people are trying to avoid them and London commuters who are experts in navigating their ways through huge crowds without making eye contact with anyone. If somehow the clipboard holder manages to catch someone (and I mean catch, because most people are walking to beat some kind of land speed record) you undoubtedly hear the following: "I would donate, but I'm late for work, sorry."

I'm not going to lie, I've used this a few times and it is the response that I'm pretty sure they have heard a million times. As you make your way past the person, you may feel relief that you didn't get stopped for long, but you may feel guilty for not letting the person do their job. You may also feel guilty because it is for a cause that you do actually support but you just feel wary about giving your personal details to a person wearing a bib. Any one of these responses will trigger a level of guilt but the word 'would' will now show you that whatever your response there was something about the situation that you were not committed to.

Should, could or would are words that tell you that what you are feeling guilty about is not important to you on the same degree that it may be important to other people. It is so important to recognise this, because you can then start to drill down into why there is this disconnect between the importance you and they place on it. You then get to decide whether they have a point. Maybe you realise that actually it is within your personal code to take that action because it does represent the kind of person you feel you are. You therefore change your 'should' into 'want'. Or you may realise that it's not important to you and then let go of the need to do it to keep others happy. If they then try to make you feel guilty for not doing it, you are less likely to give in, because you know it is not following your personal code which will feel much worse.

## Being Accountable or Guilt Trip?

If you don't do what others want you to do, then it is natural for them to pick you up on that and try to get you to change your mind. This leads to those small guilt trips that can affect not just that one scenario but all other dealings with that person. When someone tries to make you feel guilty, they are effectively telling you that you are breaking their personal code and as such, are acting in a way that they do not feel is correct. Although said in the moment, the sub text of such judgement is that they feel that there is something about your character that is wrong, not just the action that you are (or are not) taking.

It can be very subtle, but you still pick it up which is why it has such influence over you. The initial comment might be innocuous – "You're not going out like that, are you?" – but you instinctively know the sub text: "I thought you had the same taste in fashion as I do, and I would never wear that". The small observations give hints at what type of behaviour they are expecting, and it is that which causes the guilt trip. It doesn't matter what you wear, but it may matter a lot to you that this person thinks you have good fashion sense.

Guilt trips are nudges in the right direction, but you have to remember that it is *their* right direction, not necessarily *yours*. Then there are times when, instead of trying to make you feel guilty, they tell you that they are actually holding you accountable – but what's the difference? Actually, the difference is huge and well worth us exploring a bit more here.

Being held accountable is something that you should absolutely expect. It means that your own personal code is clear, and that you are taking actions which will be judged against those, and if you are found to have diverted from them, it will be pointed out for your response. The important point here is that it is *your* personal code that it is compared against, not someone else's.

Politicians during election season talk about the commitments they make if they are elected. When they are then put in the role, their actions will be assessed against those commitments, with the public telling them any time there is a deviation from that.

You are assessed by your own personal code, your personal manifesto of the type of character and behaviour you will exhibit. And, quite rightly, others will draw your attention to any action you make that contradicts that. This is a perfect example of being held accountable – it is important to know that who you want to be and who others see you as are congruent.

But when others say that your actions do not meet *their* personal codes or some abstract social norm – that is not holding you accountable but is just a plain old guilt trip. If you are being judged against someone else's standards, then not only are you no longer in control of your actions but there is no guarantee that those standards won't change the moment you meet them.

Comparing standards of other people can be confusing and frustrating. A common frustration is when you are told to be more confident, yet when you are, you are told to be less arrogant or self-important. With other people's standards, there are never any solid correct answers, so you may as well just do your own thing and not try to please them.

I just want to put one major caveat over the permission to do what you want and not try to please other people, because I don't want you to think that it gives you the green light to be oblivious to others completely. For sure, you don't want to constantly check that your actions follow someone else's rules, *but* if you are going to play by your *own* rules, you must still ensure that you take responsibility for all of the possible consequences of doing so.

If what you do impacts others, then you are responsible for that impact, and if they mention this then this isn't a guilt trip – it is holding you accountable. If you smoke, for example, you are absolutely at liberty to do so, but you must also be accountable if your smoke is affecting people around you that do not want to smoke with you. When I was younger, I remember the sight of smokers trying to wave the smoke away from their non-smoking friends, usually pretty ineffectively. But it was at least the acknowledgement that their decision to smoke should not be forced upon those who don't want to.

When you start to live unapologetically, to your own rules, you must also own the outcomes and effects of that, and be accountable for any consequence, intended or not. In many cases, someone will mix a guilt trip with an intention to hold you accountable and the only way you can hope to navigate this without taking on any unnecessary guilt is by knowing your own personal code. The more you know it, the more you can draw out the aspects that you take ownership of, but leave the guilt trip aside. You can accept that you have the obligation to avoid forcing your expectations and actions upon others, but you must also accept that the same applies to them.

In the next chapter you will see how to better understand your personal code and how to start living guilt free.

# 8:  Living Guilt Free

Throughout this book, I have tried to explain the notion of guilt, how it gets triggered, how you respond to it and ways that you are able to deal with it in a constructive way.  When used positively, guilt can help you to become the person you know that you are deep down inside, who may be struggling to be seen.  There's a good reason for hiding that person away – society trains you not to stand out, and to follow the crowd at all times.

Any time you try to change something about yourself - whether it is trying a new hairstyle, new clothes, or learning a new skill – other people are quick to first point it out and then discourage you, to get you back in line.  Instead of embracing the changes that they see in you, they will question, judge and criticise until the effort to maintain the change becomes too much.

Like the dieter who has pictures of cakes sent to their phone by their friends, when you try to change it makes others feel uncomfortable because it highlights that they are not living their unique life either.  If they don't have your courage or determination to go after it, then their next best action is to bring you down, to make you doubt your ability to get to where you want to go and even start questioning your right to want more.

Usually unconsciously, others seek to influence your behaviour to come in line with what they want you to be through the use of guilt:

**"You're going to go out tonight and leave me?"**

**"Why do you need other friends?"**

**"Have you really thought about this?"**

**"Why can't you just be happy?"**

**"You're going to wear that?"**

**"Who are you, to want more?"**

None of these are outright commands to do what they say, but they create enough doubt and uncertainty in your mind that you are most likely to give up trying to be different. Living guilt free begins with the commitment to take back control of who you are and who you want to be, being mindful and empathetic to the fact that it may upset those around you but continuing on nevertheless.

At the same time, it is important to recognise that even saying 'living guilt free' is a bit misleading, because you don't want to get rid of the compassion, empathy, and self-reflection that comes from listening to the guilt triggered by your personal code on your journey to becoming the best version of you.

If you find that you are questioning your own actions, that you are upset or irritated by something that you have done that you can tell does not represent the person you are, then that is the sign that you are beginning to take ownership of your own development and are becoming more self-aware. Any time you stray away from your true self, the guilt of not behaving in accordance with it will remind you to get back in alignment.

That is going to become the acid test of how far you are able to live guilt free, because to do so, you are acknowledging that you will need to constantly ensure you are aligned with your personal code. In a perfect world, you always follow your personal code, and guilt then never gets triggered – this should be your unswerving goal. But as a human being, it is more likely that – at least for a while – you will still get some things wrong. That's okay. The signs of progress will show by how quickly you recognise that and how quickly you then correct your course.

Even if you can see that the guilt is coming from within you, that you are not living in line with the way you want to live, you may also struggle with knowing what to do about it. It can feel unreasonable to believe that you could live any differently, which may stop you from seeing which response to make that will stop the guilt.

One of the main blocks to living guilt free is wrapped up in your self-belief – you have to believe that you can make your own choices and decisions about your life. But depending on how long you have been allowing others to control the rule book, it may feel impossible for you to make your own mind up. Once you realise that the guilt is triggered then you have to dig down into why you are feeling guilty. That includes understanding how much power you have over your own actions and the opinion you have of yourself, that may mean that you feel like you are failing in the things that you do.

The constant barrage of external guilt, judgement and expectations can get so embedded into your mind that you stop seeing it as guilt put on you by others. Instead, you start creating the story that you are failing because you are not worthy of anything else. From that moment on, every time you feel guilty, you take it as evidence of your failures.

You are worth so much more than you are telling yourself, but it takes a commitment towards self-discovery and self-love to be able to fully embrace that. Loving yourself as much as others love you may feel alien and too self-indulgent, but if you persevere you start realising that the support and courage that you willingly give others to trust themselves is just as powerful if you give it to yourself.

The first step to loving yourself is knowing who you truly are, what your personal code is – then you start behaving accordingly. Yes, other people who have been used to telling you what you should do will push back. But because you now know who you want to be, they are not as influential as they were before.

Truly living guilt free doesn't mean never experiencing guilt in the future – it is a very useful emotion to keep yourself aligned with your core values. Living guilt free is learning to recognise how and when guilt may appear, how to deal with it, and how to go through life making choices based on what you really want. Your decisions have to be what is best for you and your family, not the latest whim on social media or the expectations of family, friends and colleagues.

And this isn't about being defensive or protective of yourself, cutting yourself off from others with an "I'm all right, Jack" attitude. It is easier, when you live your own life, to be more understanding and compassionate towards others, to try to understand why they hold the opinions and judgements that they do. Many of those who will judge and criticise may not want you living your own way because it highlights to them the problems or challenges in their own lives that also do not meet up to the vision of perfection that they seem to hold up to you. By living your own life guilt free, you can show them that it is possible and start to show them ways that they can also break free from social pressures.

So how do you start living this guilt free life? The first step is to get honest with yourself on where the guilt originates and then what you are going to do with that information. If it is in judgements coming from other people, you need to overcome the guilt by pointing out alternative perspectives, other ways to look at the same situation. When you can reframe it and paint a more positive picture, it no longer triggers guilt in you and you no longer act on other people's rule books.

When you feel guilty and realise it is external guilt, you can ask yourself, *if I wanted to see this as a positive, how could I interpret this?* Being late for work may become more rest in bed, a takeaway two nights in a row is a treat for working so hard, rejecting a second date leaves you open to find someone more suitable. The more you can challenge yourself to find the positive angle, the easier it becomes.

The effectiveness of this strategy is tied to your part in every relationship or role that you have in your life. The evolution or development of how you interact with others provides all of the clues you need to understand whether the connection is well-balanced or whether it is based on some form of control via guilt. You need to review *all* of the active roles you play so that each one becomes based on how you *want* to act rather than what is *expected* of you and this can have huge implications for your ability to trust yourself and feel confident in your choices.

When you know what is important to you, what your ideas of happiness, satisfaction and fulfilment look, sound and feel like then the path to living without guilt becomes easy. It becomes easy to check what you are doing with what you want to be doing. But there are invisible influences on you all of the time, trying to move you in another direction, getting you to change direction even when it is not the direction that you want to go. These are all external influences, creating expectations, assumptions and pressures on you to be one thing that may or may not be in line with how you want to live your life.

You can't live in a bubble from those influences, so you have to work out a way to navigate your way through, honouring the relationships that you have in your life but also honouring yourself, making sure that you will also get happiness and fulfilment.

So how do you identify the roles that you play, particularly those that influence the choices you are making?

Imagine a circle in the middle of a big piece of paper, and your name is written in the middle of it.   What if you drew circles all around the outside, and in each circle, you wrote the name of someone who is important to you?   Each circle would link back to you, as a type of relationship or a role that you play: mother, father, daughter, son, brother, sister, wife, husband, friend, colleague etc.

Now think about how these people or these relationships may pop up when you are experiencing guilt.  I'm not talking here about just when those people actively make you feel guilty but your own, self-generated guilt that comes from wanting to play that role perfectly?   Whether they are openly critical of you, or you are pre-empting that criticism (easy enough to do if you have experienced it time and time again), they are influencing how you feel about yourself, good or bad.

If you were to count all of those circles, what you will see straight away is that there are a lot – and they don't even represent *all* of the roles you play.  You tend to forget about those interactions you have during the day that don't feel like they should influence you, but they do.  When you go into a shop, for example, you are a customer interacting with a shop assistant.  Or when you are a commuter, you are interacting with transport staff and other passengers.  Maybe you've read the social media feed of a complete stranger but one who you aspire to emulate so you follow them.  Each one of these is a role that you are required to play from time to time.

Each interaction you have has the potential to generate guilt because of the expectations and judgements you believe the other person has or could have of you. You can find that guilt over a really insignificant connection can have significant impact over the more meaningful relationships you have.

Each of those relationships or roles you play come with a set of expectations and if you are not conscious of this, these expectations get set by the other person and not by you. Or they can be set by what you think others want from you (but you haven't actually asked them).

Even more common, the expectations can get set by "society" that tells you what you ought to want in that role. It's not even another person but a general sense from everyone else that there is a right way and a wrong way of doing it! And remember the two golden rules – everyone has an opinion and every opinion will be different – so the chances of you being able to meet anyone's expectations are very slim and even if you do, you will be upsetting someone else.

If you don't know your own mind, what you want, why you want it and how you might get it, then you can be easily led down the wrong path and ultimately into a life filled with guilt – guilt that cannot be defeated, because each role needs something different from you and there is too much conflict to get everything right. So, you end up feeling that everything is wrong.

You should also never forget the hidden guilt that is associated with trying to keep so many roles going all at the same time. If you, like everyone else, have a large amount of relationships or roles that you play, this in itself can create a huge amount of guilt. While you may try to focus on one role at a time, you are keenly aware of all of the others that you need to also worry about. All of sudden, your energy is taken up trying to stem the guilt created for each role as well as the guilt of not paying attention to all of them at the same time.

It can feel like each role is a separate plate that you are spinning, where each one that starts wobbling or falling down feels like a failure. You need to come to the realisation that no matter how well you spin each plate, there are simply too many to keep going at all times. The best you can do is keep them all as stable as possible, so that it is easier to split your time between small adjustments for each, rather than having to try to fix many that are all spinning out of control.

To live guilt free, you will need to identify each role, and define what you want each of them to look like, so that you make decisions or take actions based on those objectives. I want you to feel that each of the relationships you have – including the one you have with yourself – are conscious, planned, positive and empowering. No more wondering if you are getting it "right" but knowing that you are. Knowing that you are doing the best you can, and that what you are doing makes you joyful and fulfilled. Knowing that the choices you make on a daily basis are the right choices for you, and because of that, knowing that you will be happier and more productive. Others will feel the benefit of that, even if initially they are really uncomfortable with you taking a stand for yourself.

## The Roles You Play

The first thing you need to identify is just how many roles you are trying to play at any one time – but I don't want you to think of your to-do list of activities and tasks. I want you to answer:

**What are the roles that are represented by how you are using my time?**

So, for example – washing the clothes. Who benefits from you doing this? Who do you show that they matter by doing the laundry? It might be your partner, your children – also yourself, because the world always feels better with clean bed sheets!! Maybe not as obvious, but it may be your mother – maybe she always prides herself on keeping on top of the laundry and so you feel that you must do the same in order to keep her satisfied that she has brought you up well. If you didn't care about keeping all of these people happy, would you still do the laundry?

Each activity that you do, however small, is really your attempt to show that you want to keep yourself and others happy and can be a strong demonstration of how you maintain your relationship with them.

Given that there are so many roles that you may possibly have, I have created a worksheet that is available to download via www.journeythroughtheguilttrip.co.uk where you will see a list of some of the most common roles you have in your life.

The first thing to notice is that there is way more than you probably acknowledged at first! That's because you don't think about all of the interactions you have over the course of the day in these different roles, but there are so many! And many of them are ones that you don't even think have an effect on you, but can absolutely affect your mood and your confidence, just as much as some of your more meaningful relationships.

Example: Go back to the customer role you play from time to time. Imagine that you get to the cashier at a shop, and you start stressing because you can't find your money quickly enough? Or you try to pack your bags really fast and they keep breaking? You feel yourself getting very stressed and fumbling over everything, but you are also aware that you are feeling quite guilty. But why? The guilt mainly stems from the fact that the current interaction contains a number of 'roles' you play with other people – with the cashier, and the other people who are in the queue behind you – and you are worrying that you will 'fail' your 'role' if you don't do everything perfectly.

And let's be honest, if you do hear any criticism, or tutting, or eyes rolling as you empty the contents of your handbag on the conveyor belt – doesn't it affect how you feel for the rest of the day? It puts you in a bad mood and that affects how you approach everything else until you can release that feeling of guilt or embarrassment. This is why you have to list all of the roles you play, because without recognising how they affect you and your mood, you can find yourself feeling guilty, but not be able to identify what is causing it.

Each 'role' you play brings with it its own pressures, expectations, and your own hopes for it. So, let's find out where you are with all of them now. For each role that you recognise in your own life, give it a score out of ten, of how you are currently doing that role. So, for example, if you are sure that your role as parent is exactly as you want, that you are able to spend quality time with your children, focused solely on them and not thinking of a million other things, answering your phone, etc., - that's a ten. If you feel that the role you play as daughter is the worse it could possibly be, and you feel extremely upset when you think about it because you immediately feel a failure – you're down at a one.

Looking at your list, how many of the roles are above 5?  These tend to be the ones that you feel fairly positive about, even while acknowledging that they could be better.  Of course, there might be more that you can do, but you are satisfied that they are doing okay.  Anything *below* 5 is the alarm bell that you feel there is an issue with that role.

Now to be clear, this is not feeling that there is something 'wrong' with the way you are handling it – many of your roles involve other people and sometimes it is *their* actions that determine this score.  So, don't go beating yourself up about low scores – it is just a sign that you are now aware of an issue, so you can take action or make a decision that makes this work better for you.

When I do this exercise with my clients, most give questions in the middle range – between four and eight.  This is because most of the time when you give it conscious thought, you actually realise that you are not doing that bad a job of it really – even when your mind make you think you are!  When you recognise how much effort you DO put into your roles, rather than how much effort you are NOT putting in and feeling guilty, you get a much fairer idea of how things are.

Once you have identified all of the roles you play and scored them, you then need to identify what is behind that score.  There will be a sense of what might be going on and it usually falls into one of three buckets:

- the time you can spend on it;
- the amount of energy that you have;
- the amount of motivation or enthusiasm for it

If you have scored a role low, you may frame this quite negatively – that you are always running out of time, that your health and energy is really low, and you keep getting sick, or that you have lost your lust for life and feel completely uninspired.  If it is a high score, you realise that you devote a lot of time to it, or that you take care of yourself and will rest in order to make the most of it, or that it is something that you are passionate about?  Which of these three factors seem to be the biggest culprit for you?  Are you constantly running out of time?  Are you struggling to physically fulfil the roles – literally running on empty?  Or is it a passion problem – having trouble getting inspired enough to take the action that you know you need to take?

Each of these influences you but each one feels like it is within your power to overcome – hence the guilt.  It is like you are not achieving something that looks like it 'should' be easy to fix.  Add to this any form of social media that tells you that everyone else has got it all together, and you may as well just dive back under your duvet!!

If you are trying to squeeze too much out of yourself time-wise, the only way you can get more time is by doing less of something else – like sleeping, or exercising, or eating.  For some reason, you can think that your needs are not important against the needs of others, but the reality is that if you run on empty long enough you won't be able to be there for anyone.

You may associate burn out with stressed executives and people in pressured corporate roles – but anyone can burn out.  By taking on too much and putting yourself under pressure to do it all perfectly, you can give yourself unreasonable goals and hurt yourself by going after them.

And even if you try to get through it all by numbing with alcohol every evening, or cake, or takeaways – that leads you to even more guilt, even more examples that you throw at yourself of you not doing very well.  And it is wrong – you are doing an amazingly complicated job extremely well – the best you can.

I know that getting 8 hours of uninterrupted sleep may seem like an impossibility, but you do need to allow your body to get rest at some point.  And you need to feed that rest – literally – with good food that provides what your body needs.  How many times have you meant to eat a well-balanced, nutritious dinner – and then end up eating a takeout as your 'dinner'?

If it happens it is not the end of the world, but you have to look after yourself inside and out – you have to nurture your body as much as your children's or your partner's or even your pet!  Love yourself as much as you love the others and understand that getting a good night's sleep is not a nice to have but is absolutely essential for you to wake up raring to go the next morning.

And that 'raring to go' feeling only really happens when you are excited and enthusiastic about what that day has in store for you. If your day is filled with chores that you hate, and activities that do nothing to keep your interest, then it will be more difficult to stay focused. From that, you will feel guilty as you won't get as much done as if you could stay on it at all times.

The biggest thief of your time is procrastination – delaying doing something you don't really want to do by creating another 'more urgent' task. If you are constantly busy but don't feel that you are achieving much, it is worth seeing what you spend your time on and whether that is helping or hindering your ability to feel good about the roles you play. Once you know where your time goes, you then need to fill it with something that inspires and excites you to avoid slipping back into delaying tactics.

It only takes small things to kick off passion that is lying dormant – a favourite photo, a reminder of a favourite holiday, or a text from the right person at the right time. These can all help you refocus onto what is important to you and your goals and to get enthusiastic. Remember the key to keeping energised is to invoke your 'want' power, not your will power.

This is also important when you consider which roles you play and the amount of energy that you want to give each. You need to balance the energy you are prepared to give with what you want that role to ideally be. Take a moment and visualise, what a ten for each role would look like. This should be your view of what is absolutely perfect – YOUR view. This is your opportunity to not worry about what other people think would work, but what you want. Now, how much energy do you *want* to put into getting there?

Here, I'm afraid you have to brutally honest – if a role is important to others but not to you, then you are going to have to own that. This is not an easy exercise and I fully appreciate that it might stir things up for you that feel big and complicated and full of discomfort and pain for you and for others. But you are not helping the situation by trying to play a role in a way that you don't believe in. Some expectations are so embedded – that of wife, husband, mother, father, daughter, son – that it can be really hard to admit that you don't want or cannot have the picture-perfect image of that role that is in your mind and all over

95

the societal assumptions. Not everyone gets a happy childhood. Not everyone gets a strong marriage.

But you don't make it better by trying to convince yourself that you do, or you can. To live without guilt can mean that you have to release the images that you have of certain roles that simply do not match the reality at all. Yes, you may feel guilty for destroying that fake image and the consequences of breaking through the illusion, but in the long run, it will do significantly less harm to you and others than continuing to perpetuate a myth.

Whether it is time, energy or enthusiasm that is affecting the way that you play the role, you now get the opportunity to reframe that into something that works for you and your personal code. If a role is important to you, you find the time, you look after yourself and you are enthusiastic about it. If it is not, you get to decide whether you want to continue playing that role – if you do, how much effort do you want to put into it, and if you don't, how can you disconnect from it.

As you begin to think about how you can get closer to the ten scenario, you will inevitably see that there is always a trade-off between them. Because time and energy are finite you have to work out the best compromise of your time so that you are able to focus on all of the things you want to, so that none get left behind. And sometimes, because everything is in balance, even though not everything is at ten, you achieve a level of joy and satisfaction with your life that you never thought possible.

Having similar scores makes you feel more balanced than having a few tens, a few 1s and lots in the middle. This is uneven, and you will constantly feel off balance and out of control. And it is when you feel out of control that you allow others to start telling you what to do.

Be careful where you are trying to justify focusing on just a few of the roles at any one time – unless it is for a very specific amount of time, it is best not to do this. If you don't fit it in now, you will find it nearly impossible to make time for it in the future. Time is elastic and hates any hint of a void or vacuum. If you say that you are only focusing on one role because it is only for a short time, the likelihood is that it will still take up all of your time and it will look like there is no way you can fit everything else back in.

A good example of where your time and priorities can become misaligned is in parenting. Because a lot of your time has to be taken up almost entirely (initially at least) on caring for your child, it is easy to let the other roles slip because you don't have time to focus on them. However, those roles still carry on, and this can play a big part in situations like the empty nest syndrome, where your children leave the family home and you and your partner can't remember how you fit together any more without them.

What you spend your time on is not necessarily a good indicator of what is important to you, but if you can try to balance things out between your time and your priority, you will find that you feel happier at the end of the day when you go to bed. If you are tired and sleepy, it will be from doing things that felt worth it.

There are occasions where you do need to give certain roles more attention (my writing of this book being one of them – my diary for when this is finished is already heaving with 'catch up' coffees, phone calls and housework). But you have to deal with them very consciously and know that you are deliberately sacrificing the other roles during that time. Keeping the compromise in mind is important in making sure you don't feel guilty for missing out on the others – it's a deliberate choice.

It is sometimes more sensible, rather than to ignore them completely, to commit to keeping a very small part of each role going, so that as your time becomes available, the roles effectively shuffle into a new order of priority. For example, many couples maintain some type of date night while their children are small for this very reason – the one day a month where they remind themselves of their relationship can help them maintain a meaningful connection, help them get each other up to speed with how they are feeling. Maybe you are a working parent who feels that the work is taking you away from being with your children – your time is being used on something that is not your main priority.

While you can always work at getting a better work life balance, you must also remember that it is all about quality if it can't be about quantity. A fifteen-minute bedtime story every night can create just as much of a bond as spending the whole day with them (but checking your work emails every five minutes). The connection is never about the amount of time you have but the emotions that get sparked at that moment.

You have to remember that if you have any type of connection with someone, you then have a role to play and obligations to fulfil. If you take your eyes off it, then the other person starts to dictate what they expect of you in the role and you feel guilty because you don't feel that you have the time (or you simply don't want) to meet those expectations. And even if they are also quite relaxed about what the role should look like, you will feel guilty because, as you are reminded the role exists, you will remember that you have completely ignored it.

## Say Goodbye to The Old You

The commitment to living guilt free is more than just learning how to not get triggered into feeling guilty. You are making a commitment to become the best version of yourself, and to be proud of who you are. You are committing to paying no attention to what the world wants you to be and instead staying true to the version of you that is created by aligning your behaviour with your personal code. You won't just have principles – you will be living by them.

This is not a commitment to take lightly. It means that you will have to let go of the expectations you have for ever being able to please others. It also means letting go of the expectations you have placed – intentionally or not - on others. Out of everything you have read so far, this can be the thing that makes you pause and really think about whether you are ready for the commitment. It is only when you think about releasing yourself from the expectations of others AND releasing others from your expectations of them that you can see just how intertwined the internal and external guilt has got. If you don't want other people to judge your actions and your life choices, then you have to also let go of feeling able to judge theirs.

This is one of the hardest steps to living guilt free, because as much as you may not appreciate feedback from others, it is instinctive for you to give it out. And that is true for everyone. You may think that you are quite open and accepting – and you probably are – but there is still something in you and in all of us that wants to be able to compare and contrast with other people. Where they appear to have something you don't, you want to feel able to comfort yourself by finding them lacking in some way.

This is a human instinct, based on your ego trying to keep you emotionally safe. Don't worry about not having what they have, it says. You've got so much more than they have, in different ways. You're not less than, you are just more than in different ways. You may not have the most expensive car, but you go on more expensive holidays. You may not be as slim as they are, but you have been in more stable relationships. The comparisons and judgements that you make on others can be justified if you feel that they will be able to judge and criticise you back. Once you commit to living guilt free, you are taking away their right to feedback on the way you live your life – and so you also lose your right to feedback on theirs.

This won't be stopped overnight – every now and then your ego will chime in with some type of judgement or comparison that may make you feel better initially but eventually makes you feels bad and guilty. Commit to calling it out when you see others do it by all means, but always remember to also hold your hand up to when you do it too.
Eventually you will find that you no longer have to consciously think about reserving your judgement of others, just as you will no longer be consciously aware of others judging you. I've been applying these lessons to my own life for nearly a decade, and although I still have a long way to go, I don't get as stressed as I used to about being what other people want me to be.

If I think back to the time of my nervous breakdown, I was fixated on trying to be the version of myself that fitted the mould that others gave me, and it physically broke me. Nowadays, I am happier with who I am, and because of that, I don't look to others for approval or permission to do anything. If what I am doing or saying hurts no-one and has no significant impact on them, then I feel free to do what I want to, and I don't watch for whether I have approval from anyone else.

In the past, I felt so judged by others, that I did a whole lot of judging myself. Nowadays I get on with my life and allow others to get on with theirs. I smile at strangers because that is how I brighten my day, but it doesn't matter to me if they respond or not. I hold doors open for people behind me because I would not like it slammed on me if I was following someone, and don't wait for the thank you that may or may not come, nor do I get cross at those who do not keep the door open for me. I allow cars to overtake me because I do not want to drive any faster, and I don't allow them to make me feel bad as they whizz past me.

To some, it might seem that I don't care, that I am somehow rebelling, and I guess in a way, I am. But I am not rebelling against each individual – I'm rebelling against the notion that my mood will be dictated by theirs. The phrase 'live and let live' becomes a mantra, a state of mind – you get on with your life and they get on with theirs. The freedom that comes along with this attitude is exhilarating. Decisions and choices that you make are not rebelling against anyone, or done in compliance with someone else's wishes, but simply because it is the right thing for you to do for *you*.

You unfortunately still live in a world that will keep trying to draw you into the judgement and comparison, so this work is not a once in a lifetime effort, but rather a relentless determination to live your life your way, and without feeling guilty. You are moulding a new you, in the image of your self-belief, your personal code and your character, exactly how you are meant to be living.

You may become unrecognisable from who you are now and that's okay – in fact, that is to be welcomed. And it would be easy to think that you are no longer burdened with past guilt given to you by other people. There is a huge weight lifted from you when you remove the guilt that is applied from others going forward, but you can't completely dismiss what you have experienced before so easily. After all, while you may commit to living guilt free, what do you do with all of the guilt you have experienced up to this point? You may not create any more, but I'm sure that one of the reasons you are reading this book is to get rid of the stuff that is already there, as well as stop collecting more in the future. So how?

Making peace with previous feelings of guilt is utterly life changing, and I guarantee that you will feel a lightness of spirit that you didn't think was possible. But you could also be sitting there right now thinking that I'm absolutely crazy for saying that you can get rid of all of that guilt – if it was that easy wouldn't you have already done it? That is true, but without knowing how the guilt has got there, the difference between guilt that moves and guilt that glues, you couldn't possibly have really known what guilt you needed to act upon and which to get rid of. Now you've done the work – you've identified your roles, you know what you want them to look like and you've been completely honest about what you want out of each of these connections. Now you have a virtual 'dump pile' of guilt that serves no purpose but to drag you down, and so now is the perfect time to dispose of it once and for all.

The first thing to do to get rid of this guilt is to lay it all out. I recommend journaling simply because you can't beat the process of getting all of those thoughts and feelings out of your head and onto a page – the process of transferring it down to paper allows your mind to finally let go of it, as well as giving you an opportunity to look more objectively at it, to assess it rather than live it. This distance allows you to be more compassionate towards yourself – you realise that at any moment in time, you are only ever doing the best you can and the choices you have made in the past were the best you could do in the circumstances. But circumstances change, and you are stronger now. Once you have laid them all out, you can see the hurtful lies and misdirections you have been telling yourself, that have been keeping you feeling less than – less worthy, less confident, weaker, more vulnerable, more guilty.

Once you have written everything down, you are going to start explaining how you forgive yourself for your past lapses in judgement and the emotional battering you have put yourself through. This writing becomes a love letter to yourself, a letter of compassion and empathy that allows you to forgive and release the guilt you have felt in the past, freeing you up to live guilt free in the future. You can explain how you have changed, how you *think* differently now, *feel* differently now. You can describe where your strength comes from, and how you see the lessons that needed to be learnt from your past guilt. These have now been learnt and you can let them go.

This process is really effective at neutralising and releasing the emotions that continue to get triggered by past events, and you will notice they almost immediately lose their potency. Once they have been made visible and demonstrably forgiven, your mind feels that it is safe to let go of the guilt and the emotion and resets itself to think in the new guilt-free way. Combined with your new technique of controlling the roles that you play and how you are going to design your life to ensure you stay aligned to your personal code and true character, desires and wants, you are now ready to live guilt free and unapologetically you.

# 9:  Living with Passion

I magine being able to live your day without feeling guilty.  Picture it, hour by hour, doing the things that you want, with nobody's opinions or advice influencing your choices.  Sounds a blessed relief especially if through reading this book you have realised just how much guilt you have been holding onto, even guilt that you didn't even know was there.  Living guilt free and unapologetically feels so freeing and light in comparison to the heaviness of dragging everything through the filter of uncertainty self-doubt and guilt.  But you have to remember that in reality, it is only really getting you back to your natural starting place.

Creating emotional and mental freedom from guilt feels new, but it is where you are *supposed* to be.  And after some time, you will get comfortable living by your own rules, and it will become second nature.  But I want **so** much more for you.  I want you to live life with real passion and energy, so I want to finish off this book by talking about how to find what you are passionate about, and how to go after it.  Living without guilt is step one on the path to true joy and satisfaction.  Living with passion, unimpeded with the guilt trips from others, is a total game changer and one that is yours for the taking.

No one is born solely for the benefit of others.  You are here to tread your own particular path.  Your individuality, your uniqueness is needed to bring vibrancy and innovation to society – you are here to do things and have experiences that only you can have.  Each day you live without guilt is great, but every day you live a life of purpose and drive, of passion and an excitement about your potential- that's perfection.  Find your Thing.  Find your passion.  Give to the world what only you can give.  No matter how much the world tells you it wants more of the same – it needs the different, the unique, the diverse.  It needs you.

Finding your passion is about turning from merely surviving to thriving. You won't be able to find it until you have got rid of the guilt and given yourself time to heal in all ways.  Stress in your body is a physical response, mainly triggered by having too much adrenalin coursing through your body and all other symptoms are side effects of that. If you are genuinely in a fight or flight situation, that energy is burned off in taking action, but normally with stress, there is no action so the chemical response just carries on because it is not getting the signal that everything is now safe.

As you reduce the levels of guilt in your life, these chemicals will start to get those signals, but then – as with any build-up of chemicals – there needs to be some time for it all to breakdown and leave your body. Once you have gone through this process, your focus may be entirely on creating a calmer more peaceful life. The eruption of mindfulness awareness in recent years has encouraged everyone to focus on times of silence and stillness and this is something that you absolutely need to incorporate in your daily routine. It provides a strong basis on which to begin to live a passionate life as it trains the body to realise that there is a calm state in between moments of the adrenalin rushes.

If guilt has triggered you into the fight or flight response and you have spent a long period of time stressed or anxious, then you have to allow that to ease off before your mind will allow you to feel that a passionate life is achievable. The reason for this is simple, although counter intuitive. If you think back to a time when you were really excited – maybe a party, a wedding, the beginning of a holiday – all of these situations also trigger adrenalin, because it is responsible for getting our body ready for action. It is your mind that ties a particular emotion to that adrenalin rush to help you interpret what it is all about. In times of stress, the perception is that the shaky hands and sweating is a bad thing, but in times of excitement, shaky hands and sweating are seen as part of the experience of being so excited. The effects are the same in both situations, but you will respond differently because of what they mean to you.

Most importantly, your body and brain can't really tell the difference immediately, so if you go from being really stressed to really excited very quickly, your brain doesn't understand the switch – it just keeps you on high alert. When I worked in the City of London, everyone talked about how they liked to work hard and play hard, which basically sums this whole thing up – by switching between the high pressure of work and high excitement of a social life, you never give your brain an opportunity to calm down. While you are wound so tightly, your brain tries to process it and find out the reason for it and will use any guilt you feel as a sign that it is something to be scared or anxious about because it is something that is not quite right.

Therefore, if you use the techniques explained in this book to release any guilt you feel, but then jump straight away into following your passions, you may find that you don't feel any better – in fact, you may feel like you've made a really bad decision, because you actually feel worse! So, before you dive straight in, I want you to take some time out to focus purely on nurturing yourself back to full emotional strength. Spend time with loved ones, catch up on getting to know each other, to reconnect at a deeper level. As you are now free of guilt around what you should eat, or drink or how much exercise to do, you will be able to choose foods that nourish, and choose activities that make you smile as much as they make you sweat.

By getting rid of the guilt, you no longer have to check what everyone else is doing before you choose for yourself, which means you can literally choose anything in the world that works for you. Eat what you want, drink what you want, do what you want only using your own personal code to help you feel good with the choices. Does this mean that you may choose foods that are unhealthy, or decide the only thing you want to do is sit in front of the television playing video games? Yes, it does. And if that is okay with your personal code, I say go for it. But you have to bear in mind that you are responsible and accountable for all of the choices you make – you can decide to do something that is considered unhealthy, and understand that by doing it you may indeed become more unhealthy – that shouldn't stop you doing it. You are master or mistress of your own life - but with that comes great responsibility.

Living guilt free does not let you off the hook from taking accountability for your actions – in fact, you may find that you think about that even more, because now you are aware that the buck only stops with you. So, if you want to do it, and by doing it you are not going to impact or harm any other person, then you can do it – but you also have to accept the consequences of it. Personal responsibility is the first thing that is given away when you start being led by guilt – you rely so much on others to tell you what you think that you stop taking ownership of your thoughts. Wrapped up in that is that you give them the responsibility as well.  But that stops today.  You want a life lived your way?  Perfect – but your way is also your responsibility.

When you start making all of your own rules, you will find that eventually that becomes your comfort zone.  And the thing to remember about the comfort zone is that you will eventually find it boring, because it is essentially just surviving.  Humans love certainty *and* uncertainty and once life gets predictable, you will search for something else – you will want to thrive.  And to do so, you will inevitably need to find your passion.

You may already know what your passion is, and it is only the presence of guilt and pressure from others that have stopped you. So, you may already feel very sure what it is that you want to focus on, which is great. After you have that pause to appreciate how far you have come, you will be able to start putting together a plan for how you are going to live a passionate life.

To start this process, finish this sentence:

**"If I could do anything, I would ...".**

This is deliberately vague, because you want to feel free to answer it with whatever comes up.  You may have very specific things, such as travelling the world, having children, writing a book, learning to ride a horse – whatever it is for you.  Spend some time imagining your day being filled with living your passion – you could even write an hour by hour description of what that perfect day looks like, and then you start mapping out how you are going to make it happen.

I have 'A Perfect Day" journal where I write a description of all of the days that I can imagine where I would go to bed feeling like I have had the best day ever.  It's a really positive book for me and keeps me going when I have the inevitable down days, where things aren't quite pulling together, and I start questioning why I'm bothering.  Yes, I have those days – my passion is helping people get rid of their guilt which is one of the few subjects that strangely, people don't like to talk about.  So, some days, yes, my work choices feel questionable.  At these times, I read through my perfect days, and see how much of them I have already achieved, and I get excited once again about achieving the rest and then I'm good to go once more.

Not everyone has only one passion though and this can sometimes make it feel that you are a bit all over the place when it comes to focusing on living with passion. But it is possible to have several passions in your life – who's to say that you can't? This is why some people like to use vision boards to explain what their perfect day or perfect life looks like, because it is actually made up of many different components, not just one big thing.

If you have only one real drive that is fine, but you may find that you can answer the question *"If I could do anything, I would ..."* in a variety of ways. That's absolutely okay – write each one down, to create your ultimate bucket list. It may seem like a lot to want to do, but you've got the rest of your life, so there is no rush.

You may find that many of the activities or things you want are connected in some way – maybe a few are connected with time with your family or focused on your personal growth. What this means is that your passion is not necessarily a thing or an experience, but a way of living your life that will bring you joy. If your perfect day is one spent with your loved ones, then there may be a huge range of things that you can do with them that help you reach that. The joy won't come from doing all of these things; the joy will come from doing whatever you want with the ones you love.

What living with passion means to you is unique to you and is fundamentally based on how you want to feel about your life, what you want your life to mean. As you grow older, you become aware of how your life has impacted others, and you start to see the legacy that you have left behind. Living with passion, therefore, is about making the most of each of the days you are here, knowing that you are creating something beautiful and making your own unique mark on the world. When you are gone, people don't remember what you had, or what you gave them – they remember how you made them feel. And one of the biggest gifts you can give others is to show them how to live life to its fullest.

I had this lesson provided to me a couple of years ago, when I was diagnosed with breast cancer. I saw it as a huge wake up call for me, as at the time I was in a job that I hated, that I knew was making me stressed and sick and yet I didn't know how to get out of it. Although I would have wanted any other escape than to be diagnosed with cancer, I also realised that it was giving me a unique opportunity to truly focus on what was important in my life and what I wanted my life to mean. Thankfully my surgery, chemotherapy and radiotherapy were all successful, and I was lucky enough to start rebuilding my life after the disruption of months of hospital visits that sap your energy and your spirit. The assumption was that I would pick up my life where I left it in the summer of 2016 and carry on as before.

However, the reality of the treatment being over and the effect on my life were very different. Being discharged from active care felt like an end to it, but you are also told all of the way through treatment that there is no day where you will be completely cured. Fighting cancer is a game of numbers and probability – you are given a prognosis instead of a cure, told that your chances of survival are hidden in a percentage number that can never quite reach 100%. I'm desperately hoping this messaging can change in the coming years and that a cure can be found, but until then, you are given reassurance and a likelihood that they have done enough to stem the tide.

From the day of your diagnosis, you lose your ability to think you are immortal and the subsequent process only confirms that. You become intensely aware that life is short and even if you live another 40 years (which, thanks to the amazing work of cancer researchers around the world, is highly likely), you still know that you haven't got time to mess around feeling bad about yourself. You become acutely aware of how many times you have stopped yourself taking action or making a decision because of guilt or uncertainty, or because others were not doing it.

As a survivor of cancer, you are never quite the same as you were before, and everybody learns something different about the process and about themselves. One thing that almost everyone I've spoken to about their cancer journey says, however, is that they no longer want to live with any regrets. As I recovered from the treatment, I asked myself what difference I wanted to make in the world. I searched for what I could do that would make me feel that I have contributed in some small way to making the world a better place.

What came out clearly for me was that I don't want others – I don't want **you** – to have to go through a similar journey to reach the point where you realise that you have to live your life your way. I wanted to help you realise that the perception of a right and a wrong way to live your life is utterly false. The world needs you to be individual and unique, so that you bring your own magic to humanity. I have spent most of my adult life talking and coaching people who feel less than, who feel that they have nothing to offer. And I realised that in almost every case, there was this belief that they were getting life 'wrong' and they felt guilty about not being what the world wanted them to be and that broke my heart.

And that's how Journey Through the Guilt Trip was born. It was my passion for helping people see that their uniqueness mattered that led me to this work and I love what I do. Because it is so closely aligned with my own beliefs and my own personal code, I live and breathe this work – it's not really 'work' for me. When I talk to friends, when I watch television, when I hear conversations in coffee shops or when I read magazines, I constantly see the essence of people being stifled in self-doubt and this false need to fit in. You were not born to fit in. If you try to, you lose your ability to find your own purpose, find your own passion that is so needed by this world.

Finding your passions in life allows you to access energy and inspiration that you never knew you had.

As you begin to live with passion, you can expect that those around you will have some opinions on that. As you will discover when you start living guilt free, initially those around you find it difficult to understand why you cannot just settle down and be happy with what you have. For many, the attraction of the comfort zone is so strong that they can never imagine being brave enough to break out of it. When they get the need for doing something wild or crazy to break the monotony of knowing what your life is like every single day, they use food, drink, drugs, sport, fairground rides to induce some excitement and uncertainty. Something like a rollercoaster can add a great deal of uncertainty into your life – but you also know that it is on tracks that mean you can't go anywhere, and that the park will have had it tested a million times to make sure it is safe.

Playing in the comfort zone isn't really challenging yourself, because you know on a subconscious level that you are absolutely safe. Using things like drugs or alcohol can have unexpected results, but again there is a sense that society knows what to do with you if you do drink too much or take a substance that affects you adversely. Even food is 'safely risky' – there are restaurants laying on bigger and bigger 'challenge' meals to stuff yourself silly with food, but again you feel pretty safe that at worse, your system will get rid of it, one way or another.

Crucially, in all of these methods of injecting some fun and excitement and uncertainty in your life, they are all possible without triggering uncomfortable or uncertain emotions. Each one is fairly predictable with how you respond to them. When you live with passion, when the things that you do in your life really, truly matter to you, then you will be riding a rollercoaster of thoughts and emotions that is so unpredictable that you are sure that there are definitely no rails keeping it all together.

To discover your passion, you have had to become more vulnerable than you ever thought possible, because you are exposing to the world the ideas and dreams that you have kept safely stored inside of you. That world may be very supportive and compassionate of you putting yourself out there – but it could also try to get you back on the rails, back in the box. To do that, they question and challenge your choice to acknowledge and share your passions.

While there will be plenty of time where you are living such a joyful, satisfying life that you simply won't care, living with passion *is* a rollercoaster – you have ups and downs. And during those downs, you will find that you feel like agreeing with them. You will ask yourself what on earth possessed you to take the leap, to show your true self, to go after your dreams. The temptation to go back to what you know will be incredibly strong, and when coupled with doubts and queries from those around you, it can be difficult to know how to keep going.

As part of the path to a passionate life, you need to do two things:

First, you need to **create that plan**, create the vision board, create the imagery that allows you every day to draw yourself back in line with your purpose and passion. Pin it to your fridge, make it your phone's lock screen – find a place that you will look every single day and put up what living with passion means to you. It could be a mantra or an affirmation, it could be a picture that incorporates all of the things that make you happy, it could be a letter to your future self – whatever you know will inspire you and keep you going on the days when the rollercoaster is throwing you up, down and around and you need to get your bearings once again.

And don't take the word 'inspire' lightly – you need to create something that triggers a strong connection or emotion for you, so that you have no choice but to act. Remember that positive guilt is your way of staying true to your personal code, and that you could recognise it because you felt compelled to take corrective action. This is the same thing. Make the connection between your passions and your personal code, so that they being to merge together.

Do this effectively, and you will find that you will feel guilty any time you try to give up on your dreams, and you will feel compelled to take the action you need. Now you are not only understanding that internal guilt is useful, but you now have a way of allowing it to help supercharge your motivation to create a better and more joyful life for yourself.

My connection between my passion and my personal code is my family, and what I want for them. I realised that, during my chemotherapy when my mood would drop, and I felt powerless, that I always took one look at my husband and my children and somehow that connection made me brave again and made me want to battle through. My desire to be a positive role model to my girls, and my desire to show my husband that I was fighting as hard as I could, were both embedded into my personal code, so that if either of those things got triggered, I took action.

During chemo, action looked like a dance around my living room with my daughters to the cheesiest music we could find. Anything to help me shake off the blues and get realigned with my purpose of staying around for my kids and my husband. Your reason needs to have the same intensity, to trigger the same type of emotional call to action. Find that, and you will find that you have no choice but to stay on track.

The second thing you need to do is to **find your support**, your cheerleaders for those times when it gets hard. You should choose your support tribe carefully and it should start with understanding what you need from them. You may already know that certain tactics to cheer you up or to motivate you work really well – and others really don't. If you can identify what other people need to do to support you, then you can ask them to come with you on the journey, to help keep you going forward even when you are telling them that you want to turn back. Do you need them to be quietly but firmly supportive? Encouraging and coaxing? Do you need someone who will tell it to you straight? Do you need someone to act like your motivational drill sergeant? What works for you?

For me, I need people who remind me of my personal code, who become the manifestation of my code and help to keep me true to it. To be clear, this isn't that I give them permission to make me feel bad. It means that they remind me that I had committed to keep on a certain track and I have somehow got diverted. Most importantly, the language they use keeps me accountable and in control – they say things such as, "Hey, you know when you did x? That doesn't sound like it is in line with how you told me you wanted to be. If you keep doing x, then y is most likely going to happen. Are you sure that you want to keep going?"

This may feel awkward at first, but it is a powerful approach. It shows me that someone else knows my personal code, and in their opinion, there is a conflict between my actions and the code. It then spells out what the likely consequences of my actions will be. But crucially, it also still gives me the option to confirm that I know it does and that I want to do it anyway. I will always have the choice to change my mind and to do things differently, but my support network reminds me to do that consciously and by drawing it to my attention, I cannot say that I stumbled into doing the wrong thing.

In the spirit of living guilt free, I also want to remind you that you are not obliged to make certain people you know part of your support team. It may be that the people closest to you are not always the best people to keep you honest – mainly because they also want you to be happy, safe and out of any kind of discomfort and pain. When you are adapting to asking more of yourself, their instinct may very well be to tell you to back away, stand down and go back to what they know you can do. They only want you to be comfortable and change is, by its very nature, far from comfortable. So, don't feel that you have to get certain people involved.

It may be that someone not as close to you is actually the best person for holding you accountable, because they don't automatically want you to stop suffering and also you probably don't know how to get around them get them to leave you alone. You will always get a certain amount of support and encouragement from your friends and family, but you may find that you have to go further afield to find the people who will not let you fail. And if you can't think of anyone that you know who that can do, then allow me to step into that position. Here is my absolute promise and declaration to you:

I know that you can do it. I know that you have everything you need to have a joyful, happy and fulfilled life. You being happy makes other happy and that is after all, what life is all about. But I won't let you doubt yourself. I will not let you listen to the voices inside and outside your own head that tell you that you are less than or that you cannot do it. I know you are more and that you can. I know that you have been put on this earth to be the best possible version of you there is and that what you are here to contribute is unique, special and desperately needed. You are not here to fit in, or to be what others think you should be. They don't know you well enough to make that call. And they don't deserve to be given that control over your life.

I will let you falter, I will let you complain, and doubt, and fret, and rejoice. I will let you cry, love, laugh, scream and sob. But I will not – **I will not** – let you feel that you have failed. If you can't quite believe that yet, if you still need help getting past the judgement and opinions that are telling you that you should give up, I'm here to tell you to keep going. Your life is meant to be filled with passion, because your life is meant to be filled with purpose and I am excited and honoured that you allow me to help you on your journey towards true happiness.

NOTES

NOTES

NOTES

NOTES

NOTES

# Acknowledgements

I have wanted to write a book for a long time and have several half-finished manuscripts, all given up on long ago. It is only with the support and guidance from some really special people now that I have managed to write a book that I am proud of.

The process of writing has turned my world upside down and I couldn't have got through it without some fantastic support.

I would like to thank my accountability partner, Sarah Dew. A brilliant writing companion and blogger for A Simple and Contented Life, Sarah wrote her book at the same time and we shared the highs, the lows, the endless coffees and the very late nights to keep on track.

A special shoutout to the Twitch community of xjemmamx, who has kept me company for hours each night, streaming and chatting and generally keeping me chilled as I took a break from writing to find out what the outside world was doing for a while.

This book is just a part of my work, and I am lucky enough to have people around me who support all of what I do. Without them I'm not sure I would have kept going but I'm very glad I did and I'm very glad I have them with me on this wild ride.

I would like to thank the numerous friends that I have met online and in real life who have taken an interest in my work and helped me feel that what I have to say is important when I really felt like giving in, with particular thanks to Jo Ferrone, Susan Francis, Sandra Sparrowhawk, Rebecca Dellar, Rebecca Ward, Harriet Starling, Natalie Costa, Deborah Goodman and Fiona Hatton. Thanks for the support, advice, occasional kick up the backside to get on and do it and for generally being my cheerleaders. I am so excited to be able to return the favour.

Thank you to the strong amazing women who always remind me that we can build each other up – Lucy Sheridan, Jo Westwood, Susie Hasler. I love you all to bits and I am so excited to be part of your journey.

Thanks to all of my friends, particularly those who kept talking to that odd, awkward young girl back at school, when no-one else would. You know that I have a tendency to go missing for months at a time – this time I promise it was for a good reason! Can't wait to catch up!

Thank you to my family who have put up with my wild dreams and have never told me I can't do or be whatever I want. I know I can be a real pain and very stubborn but I love you all.

All my love and thanks to my gorgeous daughters, Morgan and Lexi who have put up with mummy being constantly sitting in front of a computer instead of playing or watching any kind of television (apart from Strictly Come Dancing, obviously). I owe you my undivided attention and you will get it – and more. I am so incredibly proud of both of you.

Lastly, to my husband Steve, who is thankfully also a night owl and has kept me company as I write and stress about the right words to use. You have been at my side through the light and the dark, and you know you've got someone special when they only ever see what you could become. I love you always, babe.

# About Lee Lam

I'm Lee and I run the Journey Through The Guilt Trip Program. I am a qualified coach, running my private practice for over 14 years, and I am also an NLP Master Practitioner. Alongside this, I have worked in the Financial Services Industry in senior positions for over 22 years, which has been quite a ride!

I've been married for 14 years, and have 2 gorgeous children, Morgan and Lexi. Throughout my life I have had to battle my inner 'not good enough' demons, as well as pushing past people's expectations or assumptions about what I could do and I finally reached a point where I thought that enough was enough. I got fed up of constantly second guessing whether I was doing the right things as a parent, a colleague, a woman, a wife - the list is endless of rules about how you live. Enough!!

I have chosen to live my life guilt free, thinking about what I want my life to look like, and not getting swayed by raised eyebrows or frowns of disappointment that are only there because you are being braver than they are and they don't like it. I'm living my own life by my rules - and I love it.

This life involves a lot of singing, dancing in my kitchen, binge-watching endless gaming videos, fangirling over the latest superhero movie or series, reading (a lot), going to the beach as much as possible, looking up at the stars and hugging my family at all times. I go to bed feeling that I've made my day count and wake up ready to do it all again. Come and join me!

Please contact me at *lee@journeythroughtheguilttrip.co.uk* or follow me on social media:

Facebook:  @liveguiltfree
Twitter: @leelamjourney
Instagram: @leelamjourney

# Free Resources

There are some great free resources via the Facebook Group, where you can ask me questions and I will answer with quick fire FB Lives, as well as a Facebook Page that contains some more in depth video content - so there is no excuse to not start thinking of this differently - the time is NOW!

www.facebook.com/groups/liveguiltfree

The Guilt Free Friday Podcast - a free resource that delves deeper into some of the topics that get covered in Guilt Free Friday on Instagram

https://journeythrutheguilttrip.podbean.com/feed.xml

www.journeythroughtheguilttrip.co.uk

# Online Courses

The Online Course offers you an insight on how to deal with guilt trips as they come along, to get interested in why you are agreeing to things that you don't want to, and how to identify where the pressure is coming from.

It also gives you some fantastic insights into the relationships and roles that you play in your life and gets you to create each one again the way that you want it, and how to start to change those immediately.

www.journeythroughtheguilttrip.co.uk

# Group Coaching Program

I'm not going to lie, the information in the online course can be pretty intense - it's a look at your whole life, and we all do the same thing - focus on the parts that sort of work, ignore the bits that don't. So a course showing you EVERYTHING can send you running under your duvet. So there is also an opportunity to work through the online course content in a Group Coaching Program, with me and an awesome group of people who are also ready to make the leap into guilt free living. These are delivered as 5 weekly webinars, where I step you through the online course content and there is plenty of opportunity to ask questions, discuss what you are finding out about yourself, have those realisations of the blocks that have been stopping you and feel totally supported in getting rid of them for good.

In the final week, we will wrap everything together, answer any questions that are outstanding, or have crept up that you just can't see a solution for, and let the 'group mind' come up with the solution for you.

This course will take you on a journey - of self-discovery, of self-empowerment and finding your self-worth and value. And I will be there every step of the way.

It's important to me that everyone on the group program feels incredibly supported, so it is open to a limited number of people each time, and I'm opening enrolment once every quarter, so if you are considering the course but feel like you will have lots of questions, the additional investment is well worth it.

www.journeythroughtheguilttrip.co.uk

# 1 to 1 Sessions

Sometimes the guilt you feel seems impossible to shift, and you need extra support, guidance and encouragement to get through it. I am able to work with you 1 to 1 in an hour long session that will get you start to think about the role guilt plays in your life, and work with you to form some strategies to get rid of them. While a lot can be done in one session, the most effective way to begin living guilt free is an intensive program of 1 to 1 sessions aimed at supporting and encouraging you through some very sensitive circumstances. These sessions create an environment where you can be completely honest, feel completely safe, and free to explore what guilt means to you, how it is affecting your life and what choices you really want to make.

If there are circumstances in your life that feel difficult to navigate on your own, these personal sessions are a great way to feel that you are not doing it all by yourself and that someone has got your back.

I offer individual sessions, or a three month 1 to 1 program if you feel that the guilt runs deep, and that you are concerned about what may come up - that's understandable... remember, if you have been living with guilt for a long time, your ability to trust yourself and your ability to get past it may just not be there right now - that's okay, I TRUST YOU. We can work together and get rid of the guilt once and for all, and if you can't trust yourself, trust me instead.

www.journeythroughtheguilttrip.co.uk

Printed in Great
Britain
by Amazon

31556305R00078